The Passing of Temporal Well-Being

The philosophical study of well-being concerns what makes lives good for their subjects. It is now standard among philosophers to distinguish between two kinds of well-being:

- *lifetime* well-being, i.e., how good a person's life was for him or her considered as a whole, and
- *temporal* well-being, i.e., how well off someone was, or how they fared, at a particular moment in time (*momentary* well-being) or over a period of time longer than a moment but shorter than a whole life, say, a day, month, year, or chapter of a life (*periodic* well-being).

Many theories have been offered of each of these kinds of well-being. A common view is that lifetime well-being is in some way constructed out of temporal well-being. This book argues that much of this literature is premised on a mistake. Lifetime well-being cannot be constructed out of temporal well-being, because there is no such thing as temporal well-being. The only genuine kind of well-being is lifetime well-being.

The Passing of Temporal Well-Being will prove essential reading for professional philosophers, especially in moral and political philosophy. It will also be of interest to welfare economists and policy-makers who appeal to well-being.

Ben Bramble is Assistant Professor in Philosophy at Trinity College Dublin, Ireland.

Routledge Focus on Philosophy

Routledge Focus on Philosophy is an exciting and innovative new series, capturing and disseminating some of the best and most exciting new research in philosophy in short book form. Peer reviewed and at a maximum of fifty thousand words shorter than the typical research monograph, *Routledge Focus on Philosophy* titles are available in both ebook and print on demand format. Tackling big topics in a digestible format, the series opens up important philosophical research for a wider audience, and as such is invaluable reading for the scholar, researcher and student seeking to keep their finger on the pulse of the discipline. The series also reflects the growing interdisciplinarity within philosophy and will be of interest to those in related disciplines across the humanities and social sciences.

Available

Plant Minds
Chauncey Maher

The Logic of Commitment
Gary Chartier

The Passing of Temporal Well-Being
Ben Bramble

For more information about this series please visit: www.routledge.com/Routledge-Focus-on-Philosophy/book-series/RFP

The Passing of Temporal Well-Being

Ben Bramble

Routledge
Taylor & Francis Group

LONDON AND NEW YORK

First published 2018 by Routledge

2 Park Square, Milton Park, Abingdon, Oxon, OX14 4RN
605 Third Avenue, New York, NY 10017

Routledge is an imprint of the Taylor & Francis Group, an informa business

First issued in paperback 2020

British Library Cataloguing-in-Publication Data
A catalogue record for this book is available from the British Library

Library of Congress Cataloging-in-Publication Data
Names: Bramble, Ben, author.
Title: The passing of temporal well-being / Ben Bramble.
Description: 1 [edition]. | New York : Routledge, 2018. | Series: Routledge
   focus on philosophy | Includes index.
Identifiers: LCCN 2017060390 | ISBN 9781138713932 (hardback : alk. paper) |
   ISBN 9781315213385 (e-book)
Subjects: LCSH: Well-being. | Time.
Classification: LCC BD435 .B68 2018 | DDC 128—dc23
LC record available at https://lccn.loc.gov/2017060390

ISBN: 978-1-138-71393-2 (hbk)
ISBN: 978-0-367-73515-9 (pbk)

Typeset in Times New Roman
by Apex CoVantage, LLC

To Mary, Merri, and Molly.

Contents

1 Introduction   1
   1.1 The thesis 1
   1.2 My target 2

2 The Normative Significance Argument   13
   2.1 The argument 13
   2.2 Arguments for SSLW 16
   2.3 Objections to SSLW 20
   2.4 An objection to SNOG 27
   2.5 The composition objection 27

3 The No Credible Theory Argument   29
   3.1 The argument 29
   3.2 Hedonism 29
   3.3 Objective-list theories 33
   3.4 Desire-based theories 37

4 Six objections   41
   4.1 The construction objection 41
   4.2 The value for us of events 43
   4.3 The meaningless concept objection 44
   4.4 The ubiquity objection 45
   4.5 The vindication objection 49
   4.6 A life worth living 50

5   Conclusion and implications   52

   5.1 Wasted theorising 52

   5.2 Childhood well-being 53

   5.3 Public policy 55

   5.4 National prosperity 59

   5.5 Dangers of believing in temporal well-being 59

   5.6 QALYS versus WELBYS/WALYS 60

   5.7 The final word 61

Index   63

1   Introduction

1.1   The thesis

Some beings are special in the following way: they can fare well or poorly. That is, things can go well or poorly *for* them. In other words, they can have levels of *well-being*. Human beings, cats, and dolphins, most of us think, are among these beings. Trees, rocks, and cars, by contrast, are not. We might sometimes *speak* of things going well or poorly for a tree, rock, or car. If my car has just been serviced, I might say it is doing well. But here I am speaking merely metaphorically, perhaps jokingly. Things can't *really* go or fare well for a car.

An assumption of almost all contemporary work on well-being is that individuals have *three* different kinds or levels of well-being:

1) *Momentary* well-being – i.e., how well off an individual is, or how she is faring, at a particular moment or point in time during her life.
2) *Periodic* well-being – i.e., how well off a person was, or how she fared, during a particular period of time longer than a moment but shorter than her whole life (say, a day, a week, a year, or a chapter of her life).
3) *Lifetime* well-being – i.e., how well off someone was, or how she fared, in her life considered as a whole.

Some philosophers find it useful to group lifetime and periodic well-being together, referring to them as *extended period* or *diachronic* well-being, and distinguishing them from momentary or *synchronic* well-being. Others group momentary and periodic well-being together, referring to them as *temporal well-being*, and distinguishing them from lifetime or *global* well-being.

In previous work, I have argued that only lifetime well-being is intrinsically normatively significant (what this means I will come to shortly).[1] But the thesis of the present book is different, and stronger. It is this:

> *No Temporal Well-Being.* There is no such thing as temporal well-being. The only genuine kind of well-being is lifetime well-being.

Accordingly, I think that much of the present well-being literature is premised on a mistake.

I will give two separate arguments for there being no temporal well-being:

1) The Normative Significance Argument
2) The No Credible Theory Argument

In the rest of this Introduction, I will substantiate my claim that many philosophers believe in the existence of temporal well-being. This is necessary, as some who are unfamiliar with the literature on well-being have said to me they do not see the interest of my arguments, since *clearly* there is no such thing as temporal well-being. If you are already well-acquainted with the well-being literature, feel free to skip the rest of this section. But even if you do know the literature well, what I say here might prove useful as a refresher or as something to return to throughout the book to reacquaint yourself with the topic.

In Chapter 2, I will explain The Normative Significance Argument. In Chapter 3, I will explain The No Credible Theory Argument. In Chapter 4, I will consider six important objections to what I'll have claimed by then. Finally, in Chapter 5, I will summarise the arguments of the book and explain some of the important implications of No Temporal Well-Being.

1.2   My target

The idea that we can fare well or poorly at moments and over periods of time longer than a moment but shorter than a whole life is found in much contemporary philosophical literature on well-being. Ben Bradley, for example, writes:

> A person's whole life . . . can go well or badly for her. But parts of lives, or *times*, can go well or badly for a person too. Things go well for a person at some times and badly at others. When we say that someone is having a bad day, or the time of her life, we are not speaking metaphorically; what we say is, at least sometimes, literally true.[2]

Similarly, John Broome, in *Weighing Lives*, writes:

> The wellbeing of a person at a time is how well her life goes at that time. It takes into account everything that is good or bad for her at the time.[3]

> I take it for granted that we understand temporal betterness. Pleasure, for instance, is good, and it comes at a particular time. Other things being equal, it is better for you at time *t* to have more pleasure at that time than less. Eating a large cream cake is good for you now if it gives you pleasure, but it may be bad for you later on.[4]

> A person's wellbeing is made up of various components: her health, her access to material goods, her social relations and so on. Each of these is itself a complex good, with components of its own. All of these components need to be aggregated together somehow to determine how well off the person is at a time.[5]

Jason Raibley writes:

> We can ask a variety of questions about a person's level of well-being, e.g., 'How well-off is he right now?', 'How did he fare while living in Hawaii?', 'What degree of personal well-being did he enjoy over the course of his life?', and 'How good was his life, for him?' Accordingly, theories of welfare usually offer some way of understanding (a) how well-off a person is at an arbitrary point in time, (b) how well-off a person is over an interval of time, and (c) how well a person's life goes for them.[6]

Eden Lin writes:

> [It is an] uncontroversial assumption [that] you can have a level of well-being at a particular time, and your well-being can be higher at one time than at another. Your well-being at a time is not the total amount of well-being that you have accrued throughout your life up to that time. Rather, it is how well you are doing *at that time*. (A typical octogenarian has accrued more lifetime well-being until now than a typical infant has, but he may not be better off *now* than the infant is.)[7]

David Velleman writes:

> A person can fare well either over an extended period or at a particular moment. We evaluate how well a person fares over an extended period

when we speak of him as having a good day, a good year, or a good life, or when we speak of such a period as going well for him. We evaluate how a person fares at a particular moment when we say that he is doing well just then.[8]

Dale Dorsey writes:

> Welfare is at least occasionally a temporal phenomenon: welfare benefits befall me at certain times.[9]

Jeff McMahan writes:

> We must distinguish several distinct dimensions of evaluation. There is, first, the evaluation of an individual's level of well-being, of how good its present state is. We can also, of course, evaluate well-being over time: how good an individual's life is during a certain period or how good, or well worth living, the life is as a whole. If we compare the life of a person with the life of an animal, the person's life will typically have a vastly higher level of well-being, or contain vastly more good, or be vastly more worth living than the life of the animal. (This is not always true, of course. Just as the peaks of well-being accessible to a person are higher than those accessible to an animal, the depths are also deeper. A human life can be tragic, containing depths of suffering, misery, grief, and degradation, in a way that no animal's life can.)[10]

Richard Kraut writes:

> When we know what the components of well-being are, we can compare one stage of a person's life with another, and in some cases we can say that he is worse-off, or better-off, than he once was. We do this sort of thing all the time. For example, if someone loses many of his cognitive, physical, and social capacities – as sometimes happens in old age – he is worse-off than he was before.[11]

Guy Fletcher writes:

> It will be useful now to distinguish two different things that we might be interested in:
>
> > Momentary well-being: a person's level of well-being/how well things are going for that person at a time T1 or between two times T2–T3.

Lifetime well-being: a person's overall lifetime well-being/how well the person's whole life goes.[12]

Antti Kauppinen writes:

I will call an individual's level of well-being (the intrinsic value of life for her) at a moment the *momentary value* of life for her at that time.[13]

This is just a brief sample. I could go on and on.

Many philosophers use a particular sort of graph in their discussions of well-being.[14] This graph depicts a particular person's life, and looks like this (Figure 1.1):

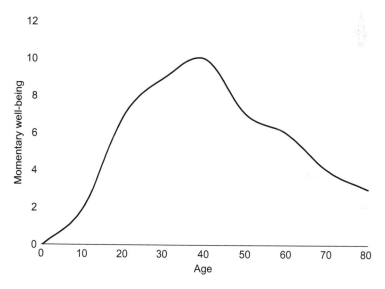

Figure 1.1 A possible particular life

Here, time or the person's age is measured on the x axis and their level of momentary well-being is measured on the y axis. In the life depicted in Figure 1.1, the person starts off (as we are all supposed to, perhaps) at a zero level of well-being, then her life gets progressively better for her over time, peaking in momentary well-being at around age 40, and then it's all downhill from there. The curve of this graph is, of course, intended as a generalisation of the periods in question. If we zoomed in down to the level of moments, we might see the curve jumping up and down dramatically as the moments tick by.

Many philosophers are *intrinsically* interested in the nature of temporal well-being (or what determines it) – that is, they are interested in this question *for its own sake*. Recently, for example, a number of philosophers have become interested in what it is to fare well during *childhood*. Samantha Brennan, for example, suggests that a childhood high in well-being is one that contains

> unstructured, imaginative play; relationships with other children and with adults; opportunities to meaningfully contribute to household and community; time spent outdoors and in the natural world; physical affection; physical activity and sport; bodily pleasure; music and art; emotional well-being; physical well-being and health.[15]

Anthony Skelton, also, writes:

> a child's life goes well when she possesses in addition to happiness certain things in which it is good for her to be happy, e.g., intellectual activity, valuable relationships and play. . . . What is non-instrumentally bad for a child is to lack these goods or to have dissatisfaction, disvaluable relationships, intellectual passivity, and so on. A child's life goes well when she has a surplus of objective goods, and it goes poorly when she has a surplus of objective evils. The very best life is the one with the greatest sum of objective goods.[16]

According to Ramesh Raghavan and Anna Alexandrova, children do well just to the extent that they

1) Develop those stage-appropriate capacities that would, for all we know, equip them for successful future, given their environment.
2) And engage with the world in child-appropriate ways, for instance, with curiosity and exploration, spontaneity, and emotional security.[17]

Finally, Patrick Tomlin writes:

> In order to see whether childhood is good or bad for children (in comparison with adulthood), we need an account of wellbeing against which to measure children's lives. The main question we then face is . . . should children's lives be measured against the same standards of wellbeing against which we measure adults' lives? Or does an altogether different standard apply? Standardly, philosophers refer to three general approaches to wellbeing (Crisp 2015) [hedonism, desire-satisfactionism, and objective-list theories]. . . . We have, so far as I can see, three options here: 1. Apply these existing theories of (adult) wellbeing to children; 2. Develop new theories of wellbeing to apply to both

adults and children which better take account of children's lives; or 3. Develop separate accounts of wellbeing for adults and children. . . . There are some quite obvious ways in which children's lives, if they are measured against adult standards, appear to be going badly.[18]

A further reason philosophers are interested in the nature of temporal well-being is that they think temporal well-being plays a key role in determining lifetime well-being. Many hold, for example, what I will call *The Construction Thesis*:

Temporal well-being is in some sense basic, and lifetime well-being is constructed out of it. We can fare well or poorly in our lives as a whole only (or at least mainly) *because* we can fare well or poorly at moments and during periods.

John Bigelow, John Campbell, and Robert Pargetter put it this way:

Global well-being depends on a person's life profile. But of course we must answer the question of the profile of *what*. The plausible and most explanatory answer is that the person has a well-being at a time – a temporal well-being. In fact the person has some level of temporal well-being at each instant of the person's life. It is the profile of temporal well-being that is needed in discussing and determining the global well-being of the person.[19]

Similarly, Dorsey writes:

Not only does welfare occur at a time in addition to occurring over an entire life, it is plausible to say that one's lifetime well-being is at least in part a function of the levels of welfare one maintains at the individual times of one's life.[20]

A major topic in the literature on well-being concerns the exact way in which lifetime well-being is constructed out of temporal well-being. As Broome asks,

How does the wellbeing that comes to a person at different times in her life go together to determine how good her life is as a whole?[21]

Now, there is a simple answer that has been offered to this question. This is *additivism*, according to which one's level of lifetime well-being is equivalent simply to the *sum* of one's levels of momentary well-being throughout one's life. On this view, a person's lifetime well-being is equal to the area under the relevant curve in the above sort of graph representing her life. The leading defenders of additivism are hedonists such as Fred Feldman and Ben Bradley.[22]

Others believe that things are more complicated than this. Michael Slote, for example, holds that how one fares during one's 'prime of life' makes a bigger intrinsic contribution to lifetime well-being than does temporal well-being at other times. Childhood and senescence, he says, make 'a rather negligible contribution to what seems to matter most in a total human life'.[23] He writes: 'within a very wide range, the facts of childhood simply don't enter with any great weight into our estimation of the (relative) goodness of total lives.'[24] Slote here is reacting to the view of many others that the temporal location of the good (or bad) times in one's life makes no difference to their contribution to a life's overall value. Following Dorsey and others, I will call this view *Temporal Neutrality*.[25] Temporal neutrality was famously held by Sidgwick: 'Hereafter as such is to be regarded neither less nor more than Now,'[26] and Rawls: 'The intrinsic importance that we assign to different parts of our life should be the same at every moment of time.'[27]

Slote has an additional gripe with additivism. According to him, the contribution of one's well-being at earlier times (say, during childhood) to one's lifetime well-being can be affected by what happens at later times (say, during one's adulthood). So, for example, he says that 'happy mature years' can neutralise the impact of 'an unhappy schoolboy career'. It can '[wipe] the slate clean.'[28]

Others have claimed that the 'direction' or 'shape' of a life matters intrinsically for lifetime well-being, where direction and shape here refer to the direction and shape of *temporal well-being*. Some philosophers, for example, hold that, other things equal – including total sums of momentary well-being – a life that goes from bad to good is higher in lifetime well-being than a life that goes from good to bad. Consider, for example, Velleman's famous description of two such lives:

> One life begins in the depths but takes an upward trend: a childhood of deprivation, a troubled youth, struggles and setbacks in early adulthood, followed finally by success and satisfaction in middle age and a peaceful retirement. Another life begins at the heights but slides downhill: a blissful childhood and youth, precocious triumphs and rewards in early adulthood, followed by a midlife strewn with disasters that lead to misery in old age. Surely, we can imagine two such lives containing equal sums of momentary welfare. Your retirement is as blessed in one life as your childhood is in the other; your nonage is as blighted in one life as your dotage is in the other.[29]

Many report finding it intuitive that the first life is more fortunate, notwithstanding the fact that the sum of momentary well-being it contains is stipulated to be equal to that of the second life.[30]

Not all philosophers, however, accept The Construction Thesis. Velleman himself thinks that lifetime well-being is determined just by the *story* of one's life, where this in turn is not equivalent to some function of momentary well-being. Consider, for example, Velleman's discussion of learning from one's misfortunes:

> Conferring instrumental value on a misfortune alters its meaning, its significance in the story of one's life. The misfortune still detracted from one's well-being at the time, but it no longer mars one's life story as it formerly did. A life in which one suffers a misfortune and then learns from it may find one equally well-off, at each moment, as a life in which one suffers a misfortune and then reads an encyclopedia. But the costs of the misfortune are merely offset when the value of the latter life is computed; whereas they are somehow cancelled entirely from the accounts of the former. Or rather, *neither misfortune affects the value of one's life just by adding costs and benefits to a cumulative account. The effect of either misfortune on one's life is proportionate, not to its impact on one's continuing welfare, but to its import for the story.* An edifying misfortune is not just offset but redeemed, by being given a meaningful place in one's progress through life.[31]

Nonetheless, Velleman considers it an interesting and important question what temporal well-being consists in.

There are further reasons for which philosophers are interested in temporal well-being. Some think, for example, that one and the same theory must be true of both lifetime and temporal well-being (i.e., that some *general* theory of well-being is true). In this case, if a theory does a good job of explaining temporal well-being, this is some evidence that it is true also as a theory of lifetime well-being. By contrast, if a theory cannot account for temporal well-being, this tells against it as a theory of lifetime well-being. Kraut, for example, thinks the fact that a *developmentalist* theory of well-being can well account for childhood well-being is evidence that it is the right theory of well-being more generally.[32] He writes:

> We make judgments about what is good for children and how well they are doing by appealing to other factors beyond their experiential states. . . . A theory about what is good for human beings should be tested in part by seeing whether it plausibly explains what makes something good for an individual when he is a young child. . . . At a high

level of generality, there is something that the good of a human child and that of young members of other kinds of species have in common: it is good for them to grow, to develop, to be healthy, and to flourish.[33]

Finally, some think that the nature of temporal well-being is an important matter for the formulation of correct 1) moral theories, and 2) public policies, independently of the role that temporal well-being might play in determining lifetime well-being or providing evidence for the right theory of lifetime well-being. Skelton, for example, writes:

> What makes a young child's life go well? What is non-instrumentally good or bad for a young child? . . . The nature of children's welfare is of great relevance to a host of moral, political, and practical questions relating to the treatment of children.[34]

Here, also, is Anca Gheaus:

> The existence and identity of [the intrinsic goods of childhood] are likely to carry important implications for what is a good childhood and for what adults collectively owe to children.[35]

And here are Alexander Bagattini and Colin MacLeod:

> Physicians and social workers sometimes seek to protect children from their parents. Yet parents often view interventions into the private life of the family as meddlesome and destructive. In such disputes, *both sides appeal to the well-being of children to justify their actions.* How should such conflicts be adjudicated? How are the choices and preferences of children relevant to tracking their interests? In the face of a plurality of interpretations of child well-being, what conception of well-being should a just state employ to craft effective laws and public policies that bear upon the treatment of children? Credible answers to these and related questions depend on identifying and assessing the significance of distinct dimensions of children's well-being.[36]

Some economists and philosophers seem even to think that maximising temporal well-being – making citizens as well off as they can be in the here-and-now – is the proper goal of public policy (more on this in Chapter 5).

All of this literature is fascinating. I have myself contributed to it, participating in this way of thinking and talking.[37] However, I now believe it to be premised on a mistake, that of positing temporal well-being. I will now commence the project of trying to persuade you of No Temporal Well-Being.

Notes

1 Bramble (2014a).
2 Bradley (2009), p. 18.
3 Broome (2004), p. 45.
4 Broome (2004), p. 99.
5 Broome (2004), p. 260.
6 Raibley (2012), p. 239
7 Lin (forthcoming).
8 Velleman (2000), p. 56.
9 Dorsey (2013), p. 151.
10 McMahan (2002), p. 159.
11 Kraut (2009), p. 170.
12 Fletcher (2016).
13 Kauppinen (2015), p. 198.
14 See, for example, Broome (2004), Glasgow (2013), Fletcher (2016), etc.
15 Brennan (2014), p. 42.
16 Skelton (2015), p. 372.
17 Raghavan and Alexandrova (2015).
18 Tomlin (forthcoming).
19 Bigelow, Campbell, and Pargetter (1990), p. 127.
20 Dorsey (2013), p. 151.
21 Broome (2004), p. 16. Broome says that answering this question is one of the key goals of his book.
22 See Feldman (2004) and Bradley (2009).
23 Slote (1983), p. 20.
24 Slote (1983), p. 14.
25 Dorsey (2015).
26 Sidgwick (1907), p. 381.
27 Rawls (1971), p. 420.
28 Slote (1983), p. 14.
29 Velleman (2000), p. 58. See also Chisholm (1986).
30 See also Temkin (2011).
31 Velleman (2000), p. 65.
32 For a related suggestion, see Sumner (1996), pp. 13–15.
33 Kraut (2009), p. 4.
34 Skelton (2015), p. 367.
35 Gheaus (2015), p. 35.
36 Bagattini and Macleod (2015), Introduction, xi.
37 Bramble (2014a).

References

Bagattini, A. and Macleod, C. (2015). *The Nature of Children's Well-Being*. Dordrecht: Springer.
Bigelow, J., Campbell, J., and Pargetter, R. (1990). Death and Well-Being. *Pacific Philosophical Quarterly* 71: 119–140.
Bradley, B. (2009). *Well-Being and Death*. Oxford: Oxford University Press.
Bramble, B. (2014a). Whole-Life Welfarism. *American Philosophical Quarterly* 51: 63–74.

Brennan, S. (2014). The Goods of Childhood and Children's Rights. In: F. Baylis and C. Macleod (eds.), *Family Making: Contemporary Ethical Challenges*. Oxford: Oxford University Press.

Broome, J. (2004). *Weighing Lives*. Oxford: Oxford University Press.

Chisholm, R.M. (1986). *Brentano and Intrinsic Value*. Cambridge: Cambridge University Press.

Dorsey, D. (2013). Desire-Satisfaction and Welfare as Temporal. *Ethical Theory and Moral Practice* 16: 151–171.

Dorsey, D. (2015). The Significance of a Life's Shape. *Ethics* 125: 303–330.

Feldman, F. (2004). *Pleasure and the Good Life*. New York: Oxford University Press.

Fletcher, G. (2016). *The Philosophy of Well-Being*. New York: Routledge.

Gheaus, A. (2015). The 'Intrinsic Goods of Childhood' and the Just Society. In: A. Bagattini and C. Macleod (eds.), *The Nature of Children's Well-Being*. Dordrecht: Springer.

Glasgow, J. (2013). The Shape of a Life and the Value of Loss and Gain. *Philosophical Studies* 162: 665–682.

Kauppinen, A. (2015). The Narrative Calculus. In: M. Timmons (ed.), *Oxford Studies in Normative Ethics*, Vol. 5. Oxford: Oxford University Press.

Kraut, R. (2009). *What Is Good and Why*. Cambridge, MA: Harvard University Press.

Lin, E. (forthcoming). Pluralism About Well-being. *Philosophical Perspectives*.

McMahan, J. (2002). *The Ethics of Killing*. Oxford: Oxford University Press.

Raghavan, E. and Alexandrova, A. (2015). Toward a Theory of Child Well-Being. *Social Indicators Research* 121(3): 887–902.

Raibley, J. (2012). Welfare Over Time and the Case for Holism. *Philosophical Papers* 41(2): 239–265.

Rawls, J. (1971). *A Theory of Justice*. Cambridge, MA: Harvard University Press.

Sidgwick, H. (1907). *The Methods of Ethics*, 7th ed. Indianapolis, IN: Hackett Publishing.

Skelton, A. (2015). Children's Well-Being: A Philosophical Analysis. In: G. Fletcher (ed.), *The Routledge Handbook of Philosophy of Well-Being*. London: Routledge, pp. 366–377.

Slote, M. (1983). Goods and Lives. In: M. Slote (ed.), *Goods and Virtues*. Oxford: Clarendon, pp. 9–37.

Sumner, L.W. (1996). *Welfare, Happiness, and Ethics*. Oxford: Oxford University Press.

Temkin, L. (2011). *Rethinking the Good*. New York: Oxford University Press.

Tomlin, P. (forthcoming). The Value of Childhood. In: G. Calder, A. Gheaus, and J. de Wispelaere (eds.), *The Routledge Handbook of the Philosophy of Childhood and Children*.

Velleman, D. (2000). Well-being and Time. Reprinted in *The Possibility of Practical Reason*. Oxford: Oxford University Press, pp. 56–84.

2 The Normative Significance Argument

2.1 The argument

In the Introduction, I said that humans, cats, dolphins, etc., can have genuine well-being (i.e., can genuinely fare well or poorly), whereas trees, rocks, and cars cannot. The latter can fare well or poorly only in a metaphorical sense. There is an important question here I glossed over. Namely, what is the difference between having genuine well-being, and having well-being only in a metaphorical sense? *Why* can't trees, rocks, and cars, etc., have genuine well-being? My explanation of The Normative Significance Argument will begin with an answer to this question.

The significance of genuine well-being

The difference, I believe, between having genuine well-being, and having well-being only in a metaphorical sense, has to do with the relevance of these kinds of well-being for two things:

1) value *simpliciter* (or *impersonal* value); and
2) reasons for action.

Genuine well-being is the sort of thing that can

1) intrinsically matter (i.e., make an intrinsic difference to the value of outcomes); and
2) provide us with, or be the ultimate source of, reasons for action, whether agent-neutral or self-interested reasons.

Metaphorical well-being, by contrast, is not this sort of thing. Call this claim *The Significance of Genuine Well-Being (SNOG)*.

Consider (i). Some outcomes or ways things could go are better than others. What can *make* things go better or worse in this sense? One thing that can do so is genuine well-being. One way to make things better *simpliciter* is to make them better *for* some being or beings. This is relatively uncontroversial.[1]

By contrast, the sort of well-being enjoyed by cars, trees, etc., metaphorical well-being, cannot make a difference to the value of outcomes in this sense. That my newly serviced car is now 'doing well' does not in and of itself make things better.

Consider, now, (ii). Agent-neutral reasons are reasons that apply to beings whoever they are and whatever they happen to care about. Some philosophers think there are no agent-neutral reasons. But if there are some, then well-being is surely one ultimate source of them. Well-being might provide agent-neutral reasons by affecting the value of things *simpliciter*. Or it might provide them *directly* (i.e., not because it makes things better *simpliciter*, but just because it is well-being).

Agent-relative reasons, by contrast, are reasons that apply to particular individuals only in light of facts about these individuals – say, in light of their relations to others, or what they happen to care about. Many philosophers think, for example, that there are *self-interested* reasons – i.e., reasons to do what would be good in some way for oneself – that are independent of, or over and above, any agent-neutral reasons one has to promote one's own well-being.[2] If self-interested reasons exist, they are reasons to do what would add to one's well-being in some way. One's well-being is the ultimate source of them.

By contrast, the 'well-being' of a car, tree, etc., cannot itself be a source of either agent-neutral or self-interested reasons. That it would be in some sense good for *my car* to get it serviced is not itself a reason to do so. This is why the 'well-being' of a car, tree, etc., does not count as genuine well-being.

The Singular Significance of Lifetime Well-Being

Let us turn now to the second part of the argument. This is the claim I mentioned in the Introduction when I said I had previously argued that only lifetime well-being is intrinsically normatively significant.

What do I mean when I say that only lifetime well-being (among different possible kinds of well-being) is intrinsically normatively significant? I mean that it is contributions only to *lifetime* well-being (rather than to any other sort of putative well-being) that can make the above-specified sort of difference to the value of outcomes and be the ultimate source of reasons. Only by affecting people's *lifetime* well-being can you affect well-being in the sort of way that itself can make things go better or worse *simpliciter*. Similarly, if there are self-interested reasons to act, they are reasons to do just what would make one better off in some respect in one's life considered as a whole. It is just one's lifetime well-being that is the ultimate source of them. Changes in temporal well-being are not sufficient *in themselves* to affect the value of things *simpliciter*, and temporal well-being is never *itself* an ultimate source of reasons for action. Call this claim *The Singular Significance of Lifetime Well-Being (SSLW)*.

It is important to note that my claim here is not that temporal well-being, if it were to exist, could not have normative significance for us. It could have such significance. It is just that this significance could not be *intrinsic*. It could have normative significance for us only to the extent that it happened to bear on our lifetime well-being. It would not be worth promoting or seeking for its own sake, or independently of any such implications.

The argument in a nutshell

If both SNOG and SSLW are true, what follows? What follows is that the only genuine kind of well-being is lifetime well-being. Nothing other than lifetime well-being deserves the name 'well-being', for nothing else in this area can make the requisite sort of difference to the value of things, or provide us with the relevant sorts of reasons.

Why is there no temporal well-being? It is because if temporal well-being *were* to exist, it could not have the sort of normative significance it would need to have in order to count as a genuine kind of well-being. Temporal well-being, then, I am suggesting, is an oxymoron. It is the idea of something that, since it is well-being, has a certain kind of intrinsic normative significance, but since it not lifetime well-being, cannot have this sort of significance.

What I am advancing is, in effect, a kind of 'error theory' about temporal well-being. When we think that temporal well-being exists we are attributing something to the world that cannot exist, since this thing, in order to exist, would need to have a significance that only lifetime well-being can have.

Note that this is not just a terminological claim, a matter of semantics – i.e., a matter of whether to use a certain word ('well-being') for a given phenomenon. My claim is different, that the phenomenon that philosophers have in mind when they talk about temporal well-being does not exist.

In the rest of this chapter, I will provide support for this argument, in four ways: First, I will give seven arguments for the crucial premise, SSLW. Second, I will respond to six important objections to SSLW. Third, I will consider an objection to SNOG. Finally, I will consider an objection to the structure of the argument itself.

2.2   Arguments for SSLW

Here, I will give seven arguments for SSLW.

The crib argument[3]

Imagine standing over your newborn's crib, and wanting things to go as well for her as possible – i.e., that she be as fortunate as she could possibly be. What are you thinking of here? What is the relevant object of your desire? The answer, it seems to me, is ultimately just her life considered as a whole. In wanting her to be as fortunate as possible, you are wanting, in effect, and ultimately, just that she have the best whole life that she could possibly have. What your mind is turned toward here is her future life considered as a whole, and you are hoping that it turns out in such a way that it has gone as well as possible for her.

Now, of course, in looking down at your newborn, and wanting things to go as well as possible for her, you might well be imagining particular periods in her life – say, her childhood, adolescence, adulthood, old age, or whatever – and having desires concerning what will go on in these periods. But here, I think, if you are like most people at such times, you would be thinking of these periods, and having desires concerning them, just for *their implications* (either causal or constitutive) for the *whole life* that is going to end up being hers. The relevance of these periods, in other words, would seem to you exhausted by their relevance for the whole life that will be hers, and *its* value for her.

It is not as if, in having desires about our newborn's future, we want her to have, say, enjoyable or carefree times during childhood *not only* because this would contribute to her having a whole life that will be good for her, but *also* because it would be good for her *during childhood*. The value for her of such times does not, in other words, seem to us to count *twice* toward her overall interests or fortunateness – once in virtue of its contribution to her lifetime well-being, and once again in virtue of its contribution to her childhood well-being.

The historical figures argument

It is common to debate the fortunateness of particular individuals in history. Was Gandhi a fortunate person? How fortunate, on balance, was Marilyn Monroe? What about John Lennon? And so on. Who were the *most* fortunate individuals in history? Who were the *least*?

In carrying on these debates, we do not form evaluations of these people's lives considered as wholes, and then *add to these* estimations of the value of various times or periods within these people's lives, in order to arrive at assessments of their 'overall' levels of fortunateness. Rather, we are interested here ultimately just in the value for these people of their lives considered as wholes.

To be sure, we are, on such occasions, interested in what happens at or during particular times or periods in these people's lives. We might even speak of their faring well or poorly at or during certain times or periods. But here we seem interested in these things just for their implications for these people's ultimate levels of lifetime well-being. For more on this, see Section 4.4.

A person's fortunateness does not seem, in other words, equivalent to her lifetime well-being plus her childhood well-being plus her adolescent well-being, and so on. Overall fortunateness, at least as we are interested in it in thinking about the lives of historical figures, seems equivalent *just* to lifetime well-being. To be interested in how fortunate John Lennon was is to be interested just in the well-being of his life considered as a whole.

Too much well-being

If temporal well-being contributed to overall fortunateness independently of its contribution to lifetime well-being, then most of us would end up with far more well-being than is plausible. A life that is 80 years long consists of 2,522,880,000 seconds. If temporal well-being were intrinsically normatively significant, then one's overall fortunateness would be equivalent to one's lifetime well-being plus one's well-being during one's first second, plus one's well-being during one's second second, plus one's well-being during one's third second, and so on . . . plus one's well-being during one's first two seconds, plus one's well-being during one's second two seconds, and so on. . . . This is highly implausible. There are *so* many times and periods within one's life that it could not be that *each* of these makes an independent intrinsic contribution to one's overall fortunateness. If it did, then one's overall fortunateness would not only be different from one's lifetime well-being, it would be *extremely* different from it. In most cases, the former would be *much* greater than the latter. Even if overall fortunateness were different from lifetime well-being, it could not be *so* very different – it could not diverge so greatly.

Merely momentary misfortunes

Recall the claim of Slote and Velleman mentioned in the Introduction that certain momentary misfortunes might not reduce lifetime well-being at all if they are suitably redeemed by later events – their negative contribution to lifetime well-being might be cancelled entirely, though they remain bad for one at the time of experience. Suppose this were true – some things can make one worse off at a certain time without reducing one's lifetime well-being at all. What should our attitude be toward such 'merely momentary misfortunes'? How should we feel about them? In particular, should we mind that they occurred?

Intuitively, if such misfortunes existed, we should *not* mind that they occurred. When we look back on them, we should not regret them one bit. And if we are facing one in the future, we should not anticipate it with any sort of dread. Indeed, it seems implicit in the ideas of these authors, in saying that the negative contributions of these events to lifetime well-being are cancelled entirely, or that the slate is wiped clean, that they think that these merely momentary misfortunes are intrinsically normatively *in*significant. If it were otherwise, why would they put it in these terms, rather than saying that the normative significance of these things is *reduced* since they no longer affect *one* source of value for one, namely, one's lifetime well-being? To say that the negative contribution to lifetime well-being of these events is cancelled entirely seems just the same thing as to say that we should not mind them.

Similarly, suppose you were *well off* in some way at a particular time but in a way that made no positive contribution to your lifetime well-being. Suppose, for example, that you were enjoying watching your favourite sitcom for the umpteenth time – by now you can recite each and every line off by heart, but it still makes you giggle. But since you'd watched it so many times before, there was nothing remotely new or fresh, qualitatively speaking, in this experience for you. Let us suppose further that, for this reason, it doesn't add anything to your lifetime well-being at all. Considered from the point of view of your lifetime well-being, this enjoyment was a total waste. In this case, let us suppose, this enjoyment is a merely momentary benefit. Should you be glad that it occurred? Did you have some self-interested reason to watch the sitcom on this occasion? This seems very doubtful. The claim that it does not add in any way to your lifetime well-being – i.e., that watching it is, from a whole-life point of view, just a waste – seems equivalent to the claim that it is not worth anything for you in any normatively significant sense, even if there is a sense in which it makes you better off at the time of experience than you would otherwise be then.

Similarly, think about what you are wanting in wanting to harm your enemy. Would you want to ruin her day if you knew that, for whatever reason, her having a bad day on this occasion would not in any way reduce the well-being of her life considered as a whole – i.e., if you knew that when future people looked back on your enemy's life and debated her fortunateness, her having had a bad day on this occasion should not be taken by these people to have any normative (in this case, negative) significance for her at all?

The trade-offs argument

Suppose one had the option of making a particular time or period in one's life much better for one, but at the cost of reducing the net value for one of one's life considered as a whole. Imagine, for example, that one could make the final stage or period of one's life much more physically comfortable, but only by doing something that would compromise a key mission or project of one's life – say, by taking a drug whose use one has opposed for most of one's life, or by cashing in on a scheme or scam one has lobbied hard against.[4]

Intuitively, if forgoing the drug or scheme is what would maximise the value of one's life considered as a whole, *that* is what one has most self-interested reason to do, *regardless of how much better taking the drug or cashing in on the scheme would make the final stage or period of one's life.*

But if temporal well-being had intrinsic normative significance for us, then we should expect there to be *some* possible increase in the value for one of this final stage that would make taking the drug or cashing in on the scheme worth it for one, on balance or all-things-considered, notwithstanding the fact that one's lifetime well-being would be best served by forgoing it.

The need for a unified account

If lifetime well-being and temporal well-being were *each* intrinsically normatively significant for us, then we might face cases where we had most lifetime-based-self-interested reason to do one thing, but most temporal-based-self-interested reason to do a different thing. How could we rationally decide what to do in such cases? Without a common currency, a way of comparing the value for one of amounts of lifetime well-being with the value for one of amounts of temporal well-being, it is hard to see how we could. I am not here claiming that it is necessarily impossible that there could be such a measure or means of comparison. But it is hard to see what one might look like.

Why is this a problem? It is a problem because it is intuitive to think that there is always (or, at least, usually) a fact of the matter about what we have most self-interested reason to do. As Bradley says, considering a view on which *one's future* is a period of time that is an independent ultimate source of reasons for action (i.e., independent of the source that is one's lifetime well-being),

> A significant drawback of this position is that it renders unintelligible a kind of question that seems perfectly intelligible. If I am in a situation

where the best future does not result in the best overall life, I might be puzzled. I might ask, 'What should I do?' I seem to be asking a question about the prudential ought. But according to this view, there is no such thing. There is prudence$_L$ and prudence$_F$. I am not asking what I should$_L$ do; nor am I asking what I should$_F$ do. I know the answers to those questions. And there is no overarching prudential ought, for the reasons just explained. Thus, according to the dualism of prudential reason, there is no sensible question I can be asking to which I do not already know the answer.[5]

To avoid this sort of dualism of prudential reason, we need to posit a single ultimate source of self-interested reasons, and this should be *lifetime* well-being.

Many additional moments

Suppose that how well off you are at a particular time matters intrinsically for your overall level of fortunateness. In this case, we get a troubling result: we could make somebody very fortunate simply by giving them many additional moments of marginally net positive momentary well-being (moments where, say, they are experiencing a very small amount of pleasure and no pain). But this is highly implausible. It is extremely doubtful that adding many such moments to one's life would add much – or, indeed, anything, depending on what these pleasures were like – to one's overall fortunateness.[6]

We can easily explain this if we take overall fortunateness to be equivalent to lifetime well-being, for we can say that adding such moments adds little or nothing to lifetime well-being. But if we hold that momentary well-being is itself intrinsically normatively significant for a person, then we seem to have no alternative but to count these many moments toward one's overall fortunateness.

2.3   Objections to SSLW

The arguments above, I believe, add up to a powerful case for SSLW. But there are some important objections that need to be considered. Here, I will look at what I consider the six most serious of these.

Non-crib-desires

The first objection I want to consider is this: While it might be true that when standing over one's newborn's crib and wanting the best for her, we tend to be thinking about her life considered as a whole (and the periods in it only as they bear on her lifetime well-being), there are plenty of *other* times in our lives when our desire for our child to do well is not a desire about her life considered as a whole, but *only* about some particular time within it.

Consider, for example, that we don't usually think about our child's whole life, or lifetime well-being, when thinking about what sort of dinner to give her, or what sort of games she might want to play this afternoon. At such times, our minds are focused solely on the here and now. This seems sufficient and right.[7]

I have two things to say in response to this objection. First, while there are of course many times when we are wanting things to go well for our child without *consciously* thinking of her whole life or lifetime well-being, at most of these times we are nonetheless *unconsciously* aware that she is an individual with an extended life (hopefully a life that will stretch on far into the future), and that what happens now or this afternoon will be an episode with a context (i.e., this larger whole). Our desires, then, even for what our child is to have for dinner tonight, are desires formed against the backdrop of this awareness.

To see that our 'micro-desires' concerning our child's life – e.g., how she is to spend her day or what she is to have for dinner – are informed by this unconscious awareness, consider how they might change if we were to expect our child not to live beyond today. In such a case, it seems, we would be likely to want very different things for her indeed – say, deep experiences of family time, rather than frivolous pleasures of watching TV or playing sports.

The second thing to say is that, even if there are times when our desires for how our child will spend today are informed *not at all* by unconscious thoughts of ours about how today's events will fit into a larger whole, it is doubtful that we should attach much significance to this. Such thinking and/ or desiring, arguably, should carry little weight in our theorising about these matters. This is because there are better explanations of our having such thoughts/desires than that we are latching on to the fact that momentary well-being has intrinsic normative significance. There are plenty of good evolutionary reasons, for example, why we should take a narrow view of some things, or focus only on the present or immediate future in certain contexts. This is often necessary, for example, in order to respond to urgent threats or challenges. If we are always stopping to think of the bigger picture, we might not have time to avoid these threats. More generally, if we are too focused in everyday life on the bigger picture, we might simply never get anything done.

By contrast, the thoughts and desires we have during the imagined moment of looking over our newborn's crib, when we are cool, calm, and collected, not having to face any immediate physical challenges or distractions, seem particularly likely to be worth something in theorising about well-being – at such a time, we seem especially well-positioned to see what really matters.

The pain objection

It might, next, be objected that there are some things we can know are bad for us *without having any idea of how they fit into a bigger picture*. Consider pain. We can know that feeling pain right now is bad for us simply because of how it feels. Feeling this way makes us worse off *in the moment*, and this is enough for it to carry significance. It is bad for us, in a normatively significant sense, by making this moment worse for us *whether we will have a future or not*.

Moreover, it might be added, when it comes to the badness for us of pain, taking the perspective of a whole life can actually be disorienting or distortive. It can make it hard for us to appreciate or properly grasp the way in which pain, intuitively, is bad for us, something we appreciate much better from a closer up or narrower perspective. Taking a lifetime view on pain, for example, might make it seem as if we have virtually no reason not to fill our child's cavity. But if we look at our child in front of us, then it is clear that we have a very strong reason not to do so – it will make her miserable and she will suffer. Of course, that reason is overridden by the stronger reason to keep her teeth healthy over the long term. But if we look at things *only* from the perspective of a whole life, then the reason not to drill seems to lose the very real significance that it has.[8]

I agree that we can know that pain is bad for us just by consulting the way it feels. But this, I believe, is not because its significance for us consists in its making us worse off in the moment. It is rather because it is just so obvious that anything that feels like this is reducing our lifetime well-being. The case of pain does not show that momentary well-being has intrinsic normative significance. It shows only how trivial the insight is that pain reduces lifetime well-being.

The best future

Suppose you have two choices:

> *Option A* will maximise your lifetime well-being.
> *Option B* will give you the best *future* – that is, it will maximise the value for you of the period of time between now and the end of your life[9] – but not maximise your lifetime well-being.

Which should you choose? Which do you have most self-interested reason to choose? According to SSLW, you should choose A. But some have found this hard to believe. 'The past is in the past', you might think, 'so forget about it! Focus only on what will make your remaining time on this planet go as well for you as possible.' Bradley, for example, writes:

> I see nothing in the notion of prudence to indicate that one should focus primarily on one's whole life. Why not care only about one's *future* well-being? If someone chooses the best future available to her, it seems difficult to accuse her of being imprudent.[10]

If this is right, however, then we do not get the link between self-interested reasons and lifetime well-being posited by SSLW.

As evidence of the claim that it is future well-being, rather than lifetime well-being, that is the ultimate source of self-interested reasons, consider the following case, from Derek Parfit. Suppose you wake up in hospital and are told that you have either had a very intense pain yesterday or will have a mild pain tomorrow. Most of us would prefer to hear we'd had the intense pain yesterday, and that no pain will be in our future. We would welcome this news with relief. Doesn't this suggest we've most self-interested reason to do what would maximise the value for us of our future rather than our lifetime well-being?

David Boonin provides a nice response to this worry. He asks us to consider the following variation on the case:

> Suppose that you have been out of town for a few days and out of touch with your family and that you are checking in with your spouse to see how your three sons are doing. Suppose first that you find out that your oldest son suffered an excruciating amount of pain yesterday, although he no longer remembers the experience. I would feel terrible if I learned this about my own son and I imagine that you would, too.[11]

Boonin goes on:

> Suppose next that you learn that your middle son is going to have to undergo a procedure tomorrow that will also be pretty painful but that will cause him to suffer only one tenth the amount of pain your oldest son suffered yesterday. If I learned that my son was going to have such a treatment tomorrow, I would certainly feel bad about it. But I, at least, would feel much less bad learning that one of my sons was going to suffer ten times less pain tomorrow than I would feel learning that one of my sons had just suffered ten times more pain yesterday. And I suspect that most people would respond in the same way.[12]

Finally, he writes:

> Suppose that you ask how your youngest son is doing and your spouse
> initially responds by saying, 'same as his brother'. Before your spouse
> realizes that this answer is ambiguous and tells you whether your
> youngest son will suffer one hundred units of pain tomorrow or suffered
> a thousand units of pain yesterday, ask yourself which answer you hope
> to hear. If you felt much worse learning that your oldest son suffered an
> excruciating amount of pain yesterday than you felt learning that your
> middle son was going to have to endure one-tenth that amount of pain
> tomorrow, then the answer should be clear: you will strongly prefer
> that your youngest son will endure one hundred units of pain tomorrow
> rather than that he have suffered a thousand units of pain yesterday.[13]

Boonin sums up as follows:

> Just try to vividly picture a person you love more than anyone else in the
> world. Wouldn't you feel worse for them hearing that they had suffered
> horribly yesterday than you would feel hearing that they were going to
> suffer only one-tenth that amount tomorrow? I certainly would. In short,
> *when we consider the well-being of those we love, and when there is*
> *a conflict between what would make their lives as a whole go best for*
> *them and what would make the rest of their lives go best for them, what*
> *we truly want on their behalf is that their lives as a whole go best for*
> *them.* . . . When you picture a loved one lying in the hospital bed, you
> have the same reaction that I have: you would strongly prefer to learn that
> the person in the bed will suffer only one hundred units of pain tomorrow
> to learning that they suffered a thousand units of pain yesterday.[14]

Why do we have different reactions here? Boonin explains:

> We often find it more difficult to think objectively about our own inter-
> ests than to think objectively about the interests of other people. . . .
> *When I am the subject of the pain, I easily succumb to a kind of tempo-*
> *ral bias in favor of the near future over the more distant future . . . but*
> *when someone I love is the subject of the pain, I seem able to picture*
> *the case more dispassionately.*[15]

I think Boonin is exactly right here. I couldn't say it any better myself.

Now, admittedly, we do sometimes think that what's most important is to
have the best future that is possible. But this, I suspect, is only because we
figure, in such cases, that the best future would also give us the best whole

life. If there were such a thing as future well-being, almost every time an option would maximise the value for one of one's future, it would also maximise one's lifetime well-being. It would only be in quite strange cases that there might be a difference.

The moment as whole-life objection

What if one's whole life *is* a moment? Then, surely, you might say, one's momentary well-being has to matter intrinsically.

In such a case, however, while it would be true that one's momentary well-being mattered intrinsically, it would not intrinsically matter *qua* momentary well-being. It would intrinsically matter only *qua* lifetime well-being – because it happened to be identical to one's lifetime well-being.

The whole-life as period objection

It might be objected that lifetime well-being is just a *kind* of periodic well-being, and so *some* periodic well-being (namely, the well-being of the period that is one's whole life) does matter intrinsically.

The trouble with this objection is that I defined periodic well-being as the well-being of times longer than a moment *but shorter than a whole life*. If you want to consider one's whole life a period, then yes, some periodic well-being does matter intrinsically. But that is something I'm happy to grant, since the kind of periodic well-being in question would just be lifetime well-being. Periodic well-being as I am referring to it in this book can never itself be an ultimate source of value or of reasons for action.

Velleman's bifurcated view

According to Velleman, momentary well-being has a kind of independent 'validity' or 'autonomy', an 'independent claim that is not necessarily overridden by that of [lifetime well-being]'.[16] He writes:

> Evaluations from the perspective of a single moment in someone's life needn't be less authoritative than those which are relative to the perspective of his life as a whole. . . . The value something has for someone in the restricted context of a single moment in his life is a value that genuinely accrues to him as the subject of that moment, even if interactions with events at other times result in its delivering a different value to him in his capacity as the protagonist of an entire life. The good that something does you now is not just the phantom of a restricted method of accounting; it's an autonomous mode of value. . . . Each moment in

a life is, momentarily, the present. And for a human being, the present is not just an excerpt from a continuing story, any more than the story is just a concatenation of moments.[17]

Velleman seems to be suggesting that there is a sense in which one's momentary well-being has intrinsic normative significance. What is his reason for thinking this? It has to do with the nature of personal identity. He explains as follows:

> The reason, I think, is that a person himself has both a synchronic and a diachronic identity. The perspectives from which synchronic interests are assessed . . . are not optional points of view that a person may or may not adopt from time to time. They are perspectives that a person necessarily inhabits as he proceeds through life, perspectives that are partly definitive of who he is. *An essential and significant feature of persons is that they are creatures who naturally live their lives from the successive viewpoints of individual moments, as well as from a comprehensive, diachronic point of view. To think that the more comprehensive of these perspectives must have greater authority is, I believe, to mistake how perspectives bear on questions of relational value.*[18]

He continues:

> By virtue of being who you are, you unavoidably occupy successive momentary viewpoints as well as a diachronic one; and just as what's good from the latter viewpoint is good for you as protagonist of an ongoing life, so what's good from the former viewpoints is good for you as subject of successive moments within that life.[19]

There are several puzzling things about Velleman's claims here. First, there is a worry about how one's *present* momentary well-being could ever provide one with a self-interested reason to act. How, after all, could we ever do what would benefit us most in the *present* moment? What we do now could influence our well-being only in future moments.

Second, it is unclear why Velleman thinks we have a whole-life perspective at all, given that he thinks we are always viewing things only from our present momentary perspectives. Shouldn't the disagreement, on his view, be between just one's perspectives at various moments, rather than between these and also some whole life perspective?

Third, Velleman's claim that 'a person himself has both a synchronic and a diachronic identity' is implausible. While we have different perspectives at different moments, I see no reason to think that these correspond to numerically different selves. It is far more plausible to think that each of us has only one self, the one whose life as a whole is ours. We shouldn't give up on this idea.

2.4   An objection to SNOG

SNOG, as you'll recall, says that genuine well-being is intrinsically normatively significant. One might seek to undermine my first argument for No Temporal Well-Being by attacking this claim. Well-being *isn't* always intrinsically normatively significant, you might say. Temporal well-being, for example, isn't intrinsically normatively significant. But it's well-being nonetheless. Temporal well-being just indicates how a person was doing at the time in question. It is a register of that, and need be nothing more.

Consider an analogy with university exams. At some universities, although you are assessed during your first two years, your ultimate university mark is determined just by the marks you receive in your final two years. There is no contradiction in this. The fact that your ultimate mark is determined just by your marks in the final two years does not show that you didn't receive marks in the first two years. On the contrary, there is still a fact of the matter about how you were doing in your assessments then. Similarly, it might be said, there are still facts about how you were doing at particular times in your life, even if these facts don't impact on your ultimate lifetime well-being.

However, the analogy is clearly inapt. Ultimate university marks, unlike lifetime well-being, are not intrinsically normatively significant.

Crucially, to show that SNOG is false requires providing some other good way of explaining the difference between the sort of well-being that humans, cats, dolphins, etc., can have and the sort that cars, trees, etc., can have. I, for one, cannot think of any other good way of explaining this difference.

2.5   The composition objection

I want to finish this chapter by considering an objection, not to either of the premises of the argument, but to its structure. This objection grants that only lifetime well-being is intrinsically normatively significant, but holds that this is consistent with its being true that temporal well-being is *also* intrinsically normatively significant. How could this be? The answer, it might be said, is that lifetime well-being is (as The Construction Thesis holds) constituted by, or made up out of, temporal well-being. As one critic put it to me, temporal well-being has normative force *that partly constitutes* the normative force lifetime well-being has.

But even if lifetime well-being were necessarily constructed out of temporal well-being, *this could have been false*. It might *not* have been true.

Lifetime well-being might have been determined or constructed in some other way. What sort of normative status would temporal well-being have had in this alternative scenario? My claim is that, in such an alternative scenario, it wouldn't necessarily have had any normative significance at all. This shows that the ultimate source of our self-interested reasons, even if lifetime well-being were in fact constructed out of temporal well-being, is *just* the lifetime well-being itself. It is just the fact that something would make us better off in some way in our life considered as a whole that is why we have a self-interested reason to do it. It is never the fact that it would make us better off at some particular time.

Notes

1 Note I am not claiming that affecting well-being is the *only* way to affect the value of outcomes. There might be other ways to do so. I have said only that well-being is one important factor in the impersonal good.
2 If there are agent-neutral reasons to promote well-being, these of course include reasons to promote one's own well-being.
3 Not to be confused with a different sort of crib argument, which has been offered by some philosophers to try to convey or explain the subject matter of well-being. I've chosen to explain the subject matter in terms of the normative significance of well-being instead (see above).
4 This might well be impossible, depending on the right theories of temporal and lifetime well-being. But imagine that it is possible.
5 Bradley (2011), p. 61.
6 Suppose, for example, that the pleasures in question are just more of the same of a particular mild pleasure one has already felt many times previously – say, a pleasant lick of a lollipop or pat on the head.
7 I wish to thank an anonymous referee here.
8 I wish to thank an anonymous referee here
9 A period, note, which might be longer or shorter, depending on what you choose.
10 Bradley (2011), p. 59. My emphasis.
11 Boonin, MS. Cited with permission.
12 Boonin, MS. Cited with permission.
13 Boonin, MS. Cited with permission.
14 Boonin, MS. Cited with permission. My emphasis.
15 Boonin, MS. Cited with permission. My emphasis.
16 Velleman (2000), p. 78.
17 Velleman (2000), p. 81.
18 Velleman (2000), p. 79. My emphasis.
19 Velleman (2000), p. 79.

References

Boonin, D. (MS). *Dead Wrong*.
Bradley, B. (2011). Narrativity, Freedom, and Redeeming the Past. *Social Theory and Practice* 37: 47–62.
Velleman, D. (2000). Well-being and Time. Reprinted in *The Possibility of Practical Reason*. Oxford: Oxford University Press, pp. 56–84.

3 The No Credible Theory Argument

3.1 The argument

The second argument I want to give for No Temporal Well-Being is as follows: While there are many credible theories of lifetime well-being, there are at present no credible theories of temporal well-being, and it is hard to imagine what one might look like. What is the best explanation of this abject failure of philosophers to come up with a credible theory of temporal well-being? Theorists are failing so badly in this area because there is no genuine phenomenon here to account for.

I will start by explaining why hedonism about momentary well-being fails. I will then move to objective-list theories of temporal well-being, and explain why they fail. Finally, I will show why desire-based theories of temporal well-being also fail.

3.2 Hedonism

Hedonism about well-being is the view that one's well-being is determined just by one's pleasures and pains.[1] Hedonism about *temporal* well-being, then, is the view that how someone is faring at a particular time or over a period shorter than a whole life is determined just by what pleasures and pains they felt then.

A number of philosophers have accepted or found attractive hedonism about temporal well-being. Bradley, for example, writes:

> Hedonism can account for temporal facts about welfare in a straightforward way: the good times in a person's life are the times when she is pleased; the bad times are the painful times. The story is simple because the time a pleasure is good for me is just the time of the pleasure, and pleasures are in principle easily locatable in time. The value of a time for a person is determined by the values of the pleasures and pains experienced by that person at that time.[2]

But this does not seem straightforward to me. The problem has to do with the meaning of a moment. In physics, a moment or instant is a region of space-time with null extension in the time-like dimension.[3] A moment, that is, is temporally *unextended*. It has no duration. If it had duration, it would involve two or more moments or instants. Not only is this the definition used by physicists, it is explicit or implicit in the writings of many philosophers on well-being. As Raibley writes, a moment is 'an arbitrary point in time', as distinct from an 'interval'.[4]

This is a problem for hedonistic theories of momentary well-being because experiences, unlike moments, *necessarily take time*. Not only is this intuitively apparent, it is confirmed by today's best science, which holds that the neural correlates of consciousness are temporally extended.[5] While pain may not be 'C-fibres firing', it almost certainly involves something *happening* in the brain. A static brain state could not be a pleasure or a pain.

How might a hedonist about temporal well-being reply? Her best reply, it seems to me, is to accept that experiences necessarily take time, but deny that a moment has no duration. The sort of moment we are interested in in moral philosophy, she should say, is simply not the sort that physicists are interested in. So, there is no problem in accepting the physicists' definition of a moment for the sort of thing in which they are interested, while holding a different definition for the sort of thing we are interested in.

How long is the sort of moment we philosophers are interested in? A hedonist might respond: A moment is *the shortest possible duration* – the theoretical lower-bound unit of time – i.e., the Planck length (i.e., the time required for light to travel a distance of 1 Planck length), roughly 10^{-43} seconds.

This proposal, however, will not help the hedonist, because the Planck length, like an unextended point, is far too brief a period of time for the relevant processes in the brain to bring about or constitute anything like a conscious experience.

A hedonist might respond with a different suggestion: A moment is *the shortest period of time required to feel a pleasure or a pain*.

But there is a different problem with this suggestion – namely, it smacks of ad hocness. Why would we be tempted to think of a moment in these terms if not because we were already tempted by a hedonistic theory of momentary well-being? Is there any *independent* reason to favour it? Our characterisation of a given subject matter should not be determined by our preferred theory. On the contrary, it should precede – and be at least some-what neutral between – the main competing theories.

There is an additional problem for this suggestion. Namely, even on it, a moment will still be *extremely* brief. While *some* pleasures or pains can be felt during such a short period, many pleasures and pains will not be able to be contained within it. Many kinds of pleasures and pains necessarily take at least a little longer. For this reason, if we were trying to say how somebody was faring at a particular moment only by looking at the pleasures and pains they were feeling over such a short period of time, very little about this person's life would get represented.

An example might help to illustrate. Consider Mary, who is 40 years old, married with two kids, well-educated, well-travelled, flourishing in her career, and a popular member of her local community. At 3.45pm on Tuesday afternoon, Mary is drinking a strong espresso and enjoying it greatly. Her enjoyment is so intense that it is the dominant thing in her psychology at this moment. All other pleasures and pains are temporarily pushed aside or not felt. On the hedonistic proposal under consideration, how well off Mary is at this moment must be exhausted by her coffee enjoyment then. This seems not to give a remotely accurate picture of the sort of thing philosophers have had in mind by momentary well-being. It entirely ignores all the other aspects of Mary's life mentioned above. It is hard to believe that the pleasures and pains felt during such a short period of time could adequately represent what philosophers have intended the notion of momentary well-being to capture.

This hedonistic theory of momentary well-being, in other words, might be adequate only if all the various features of a person's life that the notion of momentary well-being were pre-theoretically supposed to capture could find expression in this person's pleasures and pains in every shortest period in which it is possible to feel a pleasure or a pain. But this is highly implausible.[6]

A hedonist might respond that the moral here should not be that hedonism about momentary well-being is false, but rather that momentary well-being is quite a different thing to what philosophers had initially imagined it to be. Momentary well-being does not necessarily capture very much about a person's life at a particular time (e.g., her family life, career achievements, level of education, and so on). Indeed, it turns out, it need not capture much at all.

But if this is the hedonist's reply, it is tempting to think she has changed the subject. She would not be offering a theory of the relevant posited phenomenon at all – the one philosophers have been interested in this whole time – but of some other instead. Moreover, we might ask what interest this other sort of momentary well-being should have for us if it need not represent all these other features of a person's life (family, career, etc.)? What use is it?

The hedonist might respond: We should be interested in this kind of momentary well-being because it is just units of *it* that go together to determine lifetime well-being.

But there is a big problem for this response. Namely, there are many kinds of pleasures and pains that necessarily take place over a longer period of time than this shortest period. Think, for example, of the pleasures of kissing one's partner, listening to a piece of music, witnessing a beautiful sunset, and so on. Each of these pleasures requires at least some seconds or minutes to pass in order for it to be felt in its entirety. For this reason, on this hedonistic proposal, it is not clear that these pleasures would be able to impact lifetime well-being at all. They might simply be left out, which would be an odd result given that they are nonetheless pleasures.

A hedonist might respond that these longer pleasures would not simply be left out. On the contrary, their component *parts* – namely, experiential fragments equivalent in length to the length of the shortest time in which it is possible to feel a pleasure or a pain – would all count.

But there are some major difficulties with this suggestion. While it is extremely plausible that the pleasures of kissing one's partner, listening to a piece of music, witnessing a beautiful sunset, and so on, can all be good for a person to experience, it is far less clear that the experiential fragments that together make up one of these pleasures, when taken individually, can be. Consider, for example, Rick's pleasure of kissing Ilsa in *Casablanca*. What part of his pleasure of kissing her occurs at a particular moment, on this proposed definition of a moment? Is it a tingle? Is it a fraction of a tingle? Is it a fraction of a fraction of a tingle? Whatever it is, could something like *that* really be good for a person in any meaningful sense? Could it, in other words, *independently of the larger pleasure of which it is a part*, really make Rick's life go better in any way? It is hard to know. While we are assuming that there is *something* that it is like to experience such a fragment of a pleasure of kissing one's lover, listening to a piece of music, or watching a sunset, these fragments are so incredibly brief that it might be impossible for us to attend to them clearly enough in isolation from the others to know what this something is like, or for long enough to allow our intuitive faculties to reliably gauge their worth for us.

A hedonist might object that we're entitled to assume that these experiential fragments can be good for us, since we're entitled to assume they are pleasures. But there are a few problems with this response. First, are we really entitled to assume these fragments are themselves pleasures? It might be possible that a given minute-long pleasure has component parts that are not themselves pleasures.

Second, even if we assume that these experiential fragments are themselves pleasures, are we entitled to assume that they are good for us? What is at issue is precisely *whether* experiences as brief as these are – whether they are pleasures or not – could possibly be good for us in any meaningful sense.

Third, and perhaps most seriously, even if we grant that these fragments can make our lives go better for us at the time we are experiencing them, could the sum of the value of these fragments plausibly equal the apparent value for us of the larger pleasures? Is it plausible that the individual benefits afforded by each of the fragmentary pleasures involved in Rick's kiss add together to equal what seems to be the benefit to Rick of having a prolonged kiss like this? These longer pleasures, in other words, might have value for us over and above the value for us of their component parts, even if these parts are themselves pleasures. There might be some additional value for us in, say, experiencing these fragments *together, in this particular order*.

If this were not enough, there is a further problem for hedonists about momentary well-being who want also to be additivists about lifetime well-being. Suppose that 1) the shortest period of time required to feel a pleasure is one second, and 2) we are considering a life lasting only one minute. The hedonist now has two options: first, she could say that there are exactly sixty moments in this life, occurring back to back, beginning when the minute begins.[7] Second, she could say that there are infinitely many moments within the life, each beginning at one of the infinitely many different points within the first fifty-nine seconds of it. There is, I believe, a serious problem with each option.

The first option will not count toward lifetime well-being any second-long pleasure that *straddles* two of these sixty seconds, since such a pleasure would not affect this person's momentary well-being at either of the two moments.[8] Hence, this option arbitrarily privileges pleasures that happen to occur at every time during a single second.

The second option, however, while it will not fail to count any pleasure, will count pleasures many more times than a theory should. Indeed, since there are infinitely many one-second periods contained within the sixty second period, this person's level of lifetime well-being could end up being infinitely high.

For these reasons, hedonism about momentary well-being cannot be plausibly combined with additivism about lifetime well-being.

I conclude, then, that there is no credible version of hedonism about temporal well-being, and, moreover, it is hard to imagine what one might look like.

3.3 Objective-list theories

According to objective-list theories of well-being, certain things are good for us whether we want them or not. These things might include, for example, pleasure, fulfilment of one's nature, achievement, knowledge, etc.[9] We have already seen why pleasure (and pain) cannot be the sole basic ingredient(s) in momentary well-being. But what about an objective-list theory of momentary well-being that includes some of these other items as well?

Such a view also cannot be true, I believe. This is because of the truth of a view known as *internalism* about temporal well-being. According to internalism, temporal well-being is determined just by the intrinsic state of the world at the time in question. Internalism has many supporters, including Velleman, Bradley, and Broome.[10] Some philosophers are inclined even to *define* momentary well-being in such a way that internalism about momentary well-being is true. Douglas Portmore, for example, writes:

> Momentary well-being is the welfare value that some momentary segment of one's life would have if that segment existed alone, apart from any relationship it has with other segments of one's life.[11]

Here, also, is Joshua Glasgow:

> So momentary value, in being non-relational, is the value that a moment would have for the person if it existed alone, independently of the other moments of the person's life.[12]

What arguments can be advanced for internalism? First, consider childhood well-being. It is highly intuitive to think that if there were such a thing as childhood well-being, it would have to be determined just by what went on in one's childhood. Whether you had a good or bad childhood could not be affected by what happens later on, say, in adulthood or old age. Once one's childhood is done, its temporal well-being is fixed. As Velleman famously put it:

> We do not say . . . of a person raised in adversity, that his youth wasn't so bad, after all, simply because his youthful hopes were eventually fulfilled later in life. We might say that such a person's adulthood *compensated* for an unfortunate youth; but we wouldn't say that it made his youth any better.[13,14]

The same seems to apply to other times in one's life as well.

Second, if it were possible for your well-being at a time to be determined by what happens at later times, then there seems no reason in principle why it shouldn't be possible for you to have self-interested reasons *now* to do things that would make you better off only at *earlier* times. This, however, is an idea that many find it hard to accept. Consider Richard Brandt's example of the six-year-old who wants it to be the case that when he turns fifty, he celebrates his fiftieth birthday by riding a roller-coaster. Suppose this child is now about to turn fifty and no longer wants to ride the roller-coaster. It is extremely implausible to think that he has some self-interested reason to ride the roller-coaster, even if by doing so he would fulfill the desire he had as a six-year-old.[15]

Some philosophers accept that we can have self-interested reasons to do what would make us better off only at earlier times. In response to cases like Brandt's, it has been suggested that a child's desire to ride a roller-coaster at fifty is likely to be *conditional on its own persistence* – that is, any child who would want to do such a thing would want it only on the proviso that he *still*, at fifty, wanted to ride the roller-coaster. Given this, if such a child did not, at fifty, still want to ride the roller-coaster, riding it would *not* satisfy the desire he had as a child, and so would not make him better off as a child (and so not provide him with any self-interested reason to ride it). Dorsey, for example, writes:

> Much of the force of the intuition noted by Brandt, I think, derives from the general assumption that many of our desires about future experiences of this kind are conditional on their own persistence. . . . In all but the rarest cases, a six-year-old child's desire to ride a roller-coaster on his fiftieth birthday will be conditional on his continuing to desire to do so when he is fifty. And if this is correct, Brandt is of course right that we should not take this desire into account in planning for the child's future. Given the general facts of human psychology, it is unlikely that this desire will persist, and hence there would be no benefit to be gained for the six-year-old in making it the case that his fifty-year-old self actually rides a roller-coaster.[16]

What if the child's desire happened *not* to be conditional on its own persistence? What if he wanted to ride the roller-coaster on his fiftieth birthday *regardless* of what his fifty-year-old self would want then to be doing? Dorsey says that in this case, the fifty-year-old *would* have a self-interested reason to ride the roller-coaster, since doing so would benefit his six-year-old self. He writes:

> Assume that (for whatever reason) I know that my son, at age fifty, will be indifferent to roller-coaster rides on birthdays. But assume, also, that I know that my son strongly desires that forty-four years hence he will ride a roller-coaster on his fiftieth birthday. Imagine also that I can set in motion a sequence of events that will make this occur. Would doing so be beside the point? Unwise? Irrelevant from the perspective of what I, as a father, have reason to do? Surely not! Though my son will not *experience* the satisfaction of his desire, I have made a wish for his future self come true. And in so doing, I have made him better-off. From the perspective of a desire-satisfaction theory, one that accepts the resonance constraint and distance allowance, this is precisely the answer one would expect.[17]

This, however, seems like an extremely big bullet to bite. I've found very few people – either philosophers or non-philosophers – prepared to go along with it.

A further worry for the idea that what happens now can make us better off earlier has to do with self-sacrifice, and is nicely explained by Bradley in the following passage:

> Suppose Kate is a pianist, and will be giving a big performance at the end of September. She practices hard, making many sacrifices, during September; as a result, she gives a spectacular performance, and this is a very good thing for her. . . . During the concert we might well say that *all her hard work is paying off now*; we might say that it is good that she worked so hard before, or more stiltedly, that her previous hard work had *instrumental* value as a result of what is now happening. It is much stranger to say that her current performance is *paying off her past self*, in the sense that it is retroactively making her better off in the past. If Kate's performance made it the case that she was well-off while she was practicing over the previous month, it would be hard to see her practicing as involving a sacrifice of current well-being for future well-being, since her 'sacrifice' would have been beneficial to her at the very time she was practicing.[18]

Though these examples concern desire-based theories of well-being rather than objective-list theories, the moral seems clear: in order for a desire-based theory of temporal well-being to be plausible, it must restrict the relevant desires to *now-for-now* ones (i.e., desires that are directed toward the present). This, intuitively, is because internalism about momentary well-being is true.

Suppose this is right, and internalism is true. What problem does this pose for objective-list theories about temporal well-being? To see the problem, consider:

> *Momentary Earth*. Momentary Earth is a possible, but non-actual, world where all that exists ever is what exists right now on Earth in the actual world – all of the relevant matter simply pops into existence for a moment, and then pops back out again.

Now ask whether there could be any of the following things in Momentary Earth: nature-fulfillment, achievement, or knowledge.

The answer seems to be 'no'. For something to be an animal, it is not enough that it has a certain physical structure at a particular time. It must instead have a certain causal *history* – i.e., it must have come about in the right sort of way. Specifically, it must be genetically descended from animals. In Momentary Earth, where all this matter simply pops into existence for no reason and then pops back out again, no physical entity is genetically descended from anything, and so there can be no animals. Moreover, since there can be no animals, there can be no animal nature, and so no fulfilment of one's animal nature.

Similarly, there can be no achievement in Momentary Earth, since because there was no past, and will be no future, nobody in existence in Momentary Earth could be, or have been, causally responsible for anything.

What about knowledge? There can be none of this either. Even if there were beliefs in Momentary Earth, none of them could be *justified*, since they would all have just popped into existence, and so none could stand in the requisite causal relationships to past events. Moreover, few (if any) of these beliefs would be *true*, since most of the sorts of things they would be about – animals, the past, the future, and so on – would not exist in Momentary Earth.

What is the relevance of this for objective-list theories of momentary well-being? It shows that there can be no nature-fulfillment, achievement, or knowledge contained in a single durationless state of the world (or even, for that matter, a state of very brief duration). But these are the very things that almost all objective-list theories regard as central ingredients in well-being. So, if internalism about temporal well-being is true, then objective-list theories of momentary well-being entail that none of us is doing well or poorly at any time – or, at least, that there is much less momentary well-being than seems plausible.

In the actual world, it is true that some of us are fulfilling our natures, have achieved things or are achieving things, and know things, right at the present moment. But this is true only because there is a past and a future. Considering the present moment independently of the past and future, there is no nature-fulfillment, achievement, or knowledge in existence. And so objective-list theories, given the truth of internalism, are committed to saying that there are none of the key things that (they say) make our lives go well or poorly for us.

Put differently, given internalism, how you are doing right now cannot depend on what went earlier, or on what is to come. It must depend just on what is going on right now, on the present make-up of the world. For this reason, if momentary well-being consisted just of nature-fulfillment, achievement, or knowledge, then none of us could be faring well or poorly right now.

3.4 Desire-based theories

Turn now to desire-based theories of temporal well-being. According to desire-based theories of well-being, one's well-being is determined just by the extent to which one gets what one wants.[19] These theories, also, I believe, are defeated by internalism.[20]

As I claimed earlier, internalism forces a desire-based theorist about momentary well-being to embrace *concurrentism*, the view on which your momentary well-being is determined just by the extent to which the things you want to obtain at the relevant time *do* obtain at this time. But, after my discussion of objective-list theories, we can now see that concurrentist desire-based theories are, like objective-list theories, committed to saying that there is much less momentary well-being than is normally supposed (and indeed possibly none).

Why is this? It is because *the sort of things we desire for ourselves are precisely the sort that objective-list theorists identify as the basic ingredients in well-being – namely, nature-fulfillment, achievement, and knowledge – and none of these can exist in just a single moment (i.e., a moment considered independently of other times/periods). So, none of these desires could be satisfied.*

There is a further problem for desire-based theories of momentary well-being. It is doubtful that many (or any) of us have desires whose object concerns the present moment taken in isolation from the rest of our lives – i.e., for the world to be a certain way *right now, independently of past and likely future*. As I suggested in Chapter 2, even our desires concerning what we are to have for dinner tonight are had against the backdrop of an unconscious awareness that we have extended lives, and hopefully many years to come. If we believed instead that tonight would be our last night on this planet, we would likely have very different desires concerning what we are to eat, and more generally do, tonight.

Imagine going up to someone on the street and asking them: 'How pleased are you with your life *in its present form* – that is, with the state of your life this very moment, independently of what has come before and what will happen later?' Most people, I predict, will have trouble understanding your question. If they do understand it, they will likely respond: 'I don't have any preferences concerning *that*. My preferences concern what will happen to me *over time*.' I suspect that the reason we lack such desires is that we implicitly see that there would be nothing *worth* desiring in a present moment considered in isolation, i.e., independently of its context in an ongoing course of events.[21]

In summary, internalism commits desire-based theorists to concurrentism, and concurrentism entails that there is much less well-being than is plausible.

Notes

1 For more on hedonism, see Crisp (2006) and Bramble (2016).
2 Bradley (2009), p. 18.
3 See, for example, Dowden (2015): 'In physics . . . an instant is instantaneous; it is not a very short duration but rather a *point* in time of zero duration.'

4 Raibley (2012), p. 239.
5 See, for example, McKinnon (2003) and Vanrullen and Thorpe (2001).
6 This remains implausible even if we accept the possibility of unconscious pleasures and pains.
7 This seems roughly Feldman's approach. See Feldman (2004), p. 174.
8 Note that there would be no problem here if the sixty moments were the shortest periods of time possible – for then no pleasure could begin in the middle of one. But, as I've claimed, it is implausible that the shortest period of time required to feel pleasure is the shortest period of time that is possible.
9 See, for example, Finnis (1980).
10 Velleman (2000), Bradley (2009), Bradley (2011), Broome (2004).
11 Portmore (2007), p. 21.
12 Glasgow (2013), p. 666.
13 Velleman (2000), p. 68.
14 See also Bradley: 'If yesterday I desired that it not snow today, but it is snowing today, things were not going badly for me *yesterday*.' Bradley (2009), p. 87.
15 Brandt (1979), p. 249.
16 Dorsey (2013), p. 165.
17 Dorsey (2013), p. 166.
18 Bradley (2009), p. 20. See also Bradley (2016): 'Dorsey wonders why we should care whether a desire and its object obtain at the same time' (Dorsey 2013), pp. 157–158. After all, we do not care whether they obtain in the same place. A desire for something to happen far away can benefit you, according to a desire fulfillment theorist, even if you don't know that it happens. Why not also say that a desire for something at a distant *time* can benefit you? Isn't it arbitrary to say that spatial distance is irrelevant but temporal distance is crucial? The answer is no. If I want to know how things are going for me *now*, it does not seem arbitrary to confine my attention to what things relevant to my well-being are happening *now*. Temporal distance matters for temporal well-being. If we had a notion of spatial well-being, spatial distance would matter to it; but we don't, it seems. (We don't ever say 'I am well-off here' or 'my desire is satisfied here,' or 'I am better off here than there,' unless perhaps when talking about a body part.)
19 Note that a desire-based theory of momentary well-being might be considered to have at least one advantage over a hedonistic theory, namely that desires (unlike pleasures) *can* exist, and be satisfied, at durationless points. On the other hand, it is possible that desires necessarily possess phenomenology, in which case it is doubtful that they could occur at such points. I will not further explore these matters here.
20 Others have tried to show that internalism is inconsistent with desire-based theories of momentary well-being. See, for example, Bradley (2009), pp. 18–25. But my argument will be quite different.
21 If we have any such desires for the present moment taken in isolation, it is probably just a desire to feel as little pain as possible.

References

Bradley, B. (2009). *Well-Being and Death*. Oxford: Oxford University Press.
Bradley, B. (2011). Narrativity, Freedom, and Redeeming the Past. *Social Theory and Practice* 37: 47–62.

Bradley, B. (2016). Well-Being at a Time. *Philosophic Exchange* 45(1).

Bramble, B. (2016). A New Defense of Hedonism About Well-Being. *Ergo* 3(4). DOI: http://dx.doi.org/10.3998/ergo.12405314.0003.004

Brandt, R. (1979). *A Theory of the Good and the Right*. Oxford: Oxford University Press.

Broome, J. (2004). *Weighing Lives*. Oxford: Oxford University Press.

Crisp, R. (2006). *Reasons and the Good*. New York: Oxford University Press.

Dorsey, D. (2013). Desire-Satisfaction and Welfare as Temporal. *Ethical Theory and Moral Practice* 16: 151–171.

Dowden, B. (2015). Time (Time Supplement). In: *The Internet Encyclopedia of Philosophy*. www.iep.utm.edu/time-sup/

Feldman, F. (2004). *Pleasure and the Good Life*. New York: Oxford University Press.

Finnis, J. (1980). *Natural Law and Natural Rights*. Oxford: Oxford University Press.

Glasgow, J. (2013). The Shape of a Life and the Value of Loss and Gain. *Philosophical Studies* 162: 665–682.

McKinnon, N. (2003). Presentism and Consciousness. *Australasian Journal of Philosophy* 81(3): 305–323.

Portmore, D. (2007). Well-Being, Achievement, and Self-Sacrifice. *Journal of Ethics & Social Philosophy* 2(2).

Raibley, J. (2012). Welfare Over Time and the Case for Holism. *Philosophical Papers* 41(2): 239–265.

Vanrullen, R. and Thorpe, S.J. (2001). The Time Course of Visual Processing: From Early Perception to Decision-Making. *Journal of Cognitive Neuroscience* 13(4): 454–461.

Velleman, D. (2000). Well-being and Time. Reprinted in *The Possibility of Practical Reason*. Oxford: Oxford University Press, pp. 56–84.

4 Six objections

In this section, I will consider six important objections to what I've claimed so far.

4.1 The construction objection

It might be suggested that what I've said so far cannot be right because without temporal well-being, there could be no lifetime well-being. This is because, as The Construction Thesis holds, lifetime well-being is constructed out of units of temporal well-being. If nothing goes well or badly for us at times, then nothing could go well or badly for us in our lives considered as wholes. Indeed, it might be suggested, we can be sure that temporal well-being exists, since we can infer its existence from the patent existence of lifetime well-being.

But I do not think we need posit temporal well-being in order to account for lifetime well-being. There are plenty of credible theories of lifetime well-being that make no reference at all to temporal well-being.

Consider, first, a hedonistic theory of lifetime well-being. A hedonist needn't hold that lifetime well-being is the sum of momentary well-being, where momentary well-being is determined just by pleasures and pains. Instead, she can say that lifetime well-being is determined *directly* by our pleasures and pains. There is no need for an intermediary such as momentary well-being.

Indeed, a hedonism like this would not face the sort of problems I sketched for hedonism about momentary well-being in Chapter 3. It need have nothing to say about the meaning of a moment. The duration of a pleasure is relevant, on this theory, only to how much this pleasure adds to lifetime well-being (it might be, for example, that the longer a pleasure lasts, the more it contributes to lifetime well-being). Similarly, this form of hedonism is untroubled by the issues of aggregation I raised. As I suggested earlier, if lifetime well-being were the sum of momentary well-being, where momentary well-being is determined just by one's pleasures and pains at the moment in question, then we face worries about 1) how to identify the moments that are to come together to constitute lifetime well-being, and 2) what to say about pleasures that do not fit neatly into any of these moments, but straddle them. But on the version of hedonism I'm proposing now, there are no worries here. Since pleasures count directly toward lifetime well-being, we can say that they count toward lifetime well-being *wherever* they occur in a life.

It might be objected that a pain is simply too small a part of a whole life to have a *direct* negative impact on one's lifetime well-being. Instead, its negative impact must be on some smaller slice of one's life, and only in virtue of *that* on the life as a whole. But it is important to remember that a whole life is just a very long period.[1] If one finds it plausible that an event like a pain can directly reduce periodic well-being, then one should also be okay with the idea that a pain can directly reduce lifetime well-being.

Consider, next, desire-based theories of lifetime well-being. A desire-based theorist has at least two decent options available to her that do not require positing temporal well-being. First, she could say that lifetime well-being is determined just by the amount of desire-satisfaction accrued during one's life. On this view, getting what one wants does not make one better off in one's life considered as a whole *by making one better off at some time*. Rather, it makes one better off in one's life considered as a whole *directly*.

This view still faces the worry that it is counterintuitive that, in Brandt's case, for example, it benefits the person to ride the roller-coaster. But the problem is less severe, for there is no need to locate this benefit at some time – i.e., there is no need to say that riding the roller-coaster improves either this person's childhood or his life as a fifty-year-old. If one is prepared to accept that it benefits him, one at least does not need to say that it improves his life at either of these times (that, after all, is the *most* counterintuitive part of the worry). In any case, this desire-based theorist of lifetime well-being could hold concurrentism, and say that desire-satisfactions add to one's lifetime well-being only if one is getting what one wants while one wants it.

A desire-based theorist of lifetime well-being can avoid these tricky problems of changing desires altogether simply by claiming that lifetime well-being is determined, not by individual desire-satisfactions, but just by the preferences that one's fully idealised self would have between the various different possible whole lives that could be one's own. On this theory, how good one's actual whole life was for one, is a matter of how high up this life appears in the preference-ranking one would give of all one's possible lives, if one were fully informed of all these options, feeling calm, etc.[2] Here, again, there is no need to posit anything like temporal well-being.

Finally, what about objective-list theories? Objective-list theorists can say simply that lifetime well-being is determined just by the extent to which a person felt pleasure, fulfilled her nature, achieved things, attained knowledge, etc., during her lifetime. There is no need to say that these things benefit us at particular times.

While it is indeed true that *times* – moments and periods – are necessary for there to be lifetime well-being, temporal *well-being* is unnecessary for this. It is entirely possible – indeed, quite plausible – that the basic building blocks of lifetime well-being are not units of temporal well-being, but rather, say, pleasures, desire-satisfactions, achievements, etc., themselves.

4.2　The value for us of events

Suppose it is accepted that there can be lifetime well-being without temporal well-being. What about the value for us of *events*? How can events – such as, to take Bradley's favourite examples, one's getting sick or injured – be good or bad for us without making us better or worse off at particular times? Bradley writes:

> Consider an ordinary case of badness. In the summer of 2006 I badly stubbed my left pinky toe while walking in the dark. It hurt a lot for a little while. It hurt a fair bit for several days afterwards. After about a week, it pretty much stopped hurting. At what times was the toe-stubbing bad for me? This question seems to have an obvious answer. It was worst for me for a little while after it happened. It was bad for me, but somewhat less bad, for the ensuing week. It is not bad for me now at all. The duration of the harm is limited and, in principle, easily locatable. . . . The toe-stubbing is bad [for me] because of what happens at those times after the toe-stubbing. *If not for the fact that it caused me to suffer harm at those later times, the toe-stubbing would not have been bad [for me]. This suggests that it is essential, at least to a certain sort of harm, that it be bad [for one] at a particular time.*[3]

Some philosophers, including Bradley, are tempted by the view that *anything*, in order to harm us, must make us worse off at some time. This is why so many have found it puzzling how *death* can harm us, since it can seem as though there is no time at which one can be made worse off by one's own death.[4]

However, it seems to me that we can easily account for the value for us of events without positing temporal well-being. We say that events benefit or harm us just by reducing our lifetime well-being – i.e., without making us better or worse off at any time. They might do this either *directly* themselves, or in virtue of causing things (like, in the toe-stubbing case, some pain) that in turn directly affect our lifetime well-being. Again, there is no need for an intermediary.

Of course, there are times at which, say, sicknesses and injuries *occur*. Moreover, there are times at which *the things that sicknesses and injuries cause in virtue of which they are bad for us* (e.g., pains, desire-frustration, or whatever it might be) – occur. But it doesn't follow, and I see no reason to believe, that these consequences make us worse off *at these times* (where by this is meant a reduction in the sort of thing philosophers have in mind by temporal well-being).

Bradley is right that we can meaningfully ask, 'When was the toe-stubbing bad for me?' He might also be right that the answer is: 'at those times when I was hurting as a result of it'. But there is no reason to think that in saying such a thing we are referring to the effects of the toe-stubbing on something like temporal well-being. To say that the toe-stubbing was bad for me at these times might be to say just that *it was at these times that the toe-stubbing had consequences (say, pains) that themselves directly reduced my lifetime well-being*.

4.3   The meaningless concept objection

It might be objected that I am making a lot of claims about temporal well-being for somebody who thinks there is no such thing. Don't my words betray me? Surely I do believe in temporal well-being, after all. How could all these claims about temporal well-being be true if there were no such thing? Consider, for example, my claim that internalism about momentary well-being is true. How could it be true that momentary well-being is determined just by the intrinsic state of the world at the time in question, if there is no such thing as momentary well-being (indeed, if the very idea of momentary well-being is confused)? Or consider my many references in Chapter 2 to temporal well-being, and my claim that it lacks intrinsic normative significance. Wasn't I, in effect, saying that there is this thing, temporal well-being, which lacks intrinsic normative significance?

However, as I hope should be obvious by now, I have not claimed that temporal well-being exists and 1) is determined just by the intrinsic state of the world at the time in question, and 2) lacks intrinsic normative significance. Rather, my claim has been, strictly speaking, that *if* temporal well-being were to exist, it would have to be determined just by the intrinsic state of the world at the time in question, and would lack intrinsic normative significance.

While it is true that the notion of temporal well-being is ultimately conceptually confused, it does have some content. Temporal well-being is, for example, supposed to be a kind of well-being, and so for something to be temporal well-being it would have to be (given the nature of well-being) something that has intrinsic normative significance. So, while there is no such thing as temporal well-being, we can, in this way, meaningfully think about what it would have to be like in order to exist.

4.4 The ubiquity objection

Suppose I am right and there is no such thing as temporal well-being. In this case, what are we all doing when we say things like 'Things are going well for me right now', 'I had a good day today', 'How is Bill doing these days?', 'Ellen had a blessed childhood', and so on? As Bradley says,

> talk of times being good or bad for people is ubiquitous; some nostalgic types say that their college years were the best years of their lives; we often talk of someone who is going through a bad time right now.[5]

How can we account for such talk if there is no such thing as temporal well-being? Am I suggesting that at all these times we are talking nonsense?

Bradley himself expresses something like this worry in the following:

> It is a mistake to focus *exclusively* on whole lives. We should also care about welfare levels at particular times and at intervals of time smaller than a whole life. Consider, for example, the famous question Ronald Reagan asked the American public in October 1980: 'Ask yourself: Are you better off than you were four years ago?' This is a question about temporal well-being. If all we have is a theory about welfare in a whole life, we cannot answer Reagan's question.[6]

My response to this important objection is that most of the time when we are engaging in this kind of talk, we *are* making sense, but we are not making attributions of (or asking about) the sort of thing that philosophers have in mind by temporal well-being. We are doing something else. Such language should not be interpreted literally, but calls for a subtler analysis. In the rest of this section, I will explain some of the main things we *are* doing in our talk about how well off people are at times and over periods of time.

Talk of periodic well-being

One thing, I think, we are often doing when we say things like 'Ellen had a blessed childhood' is commenting on the intrinsic contributions of the events and experiences of the relevant period to a person's *lifetime* well-being. So, for example, if I say that I had a great time during college, or that my college years were the best of my life, I might be saying that there were certain events or experiences then – for example, romantic or sexual encounters, experiences of discovering great music or literature, travels or adventures with friends, intellectual stimulation, and so on – that will, at the end of the day, have been among the greatest intrinsic contributors to my lifetime well-being. The events and experiences of these years will make a greater intrinsic contribution to my ultimate level of lifetime well-being than those of most or all other times in my life.

Alternatively, I might be saying, not that the events and experiences of the relevant period will contribute more to my lifetime well-being than those of other periods of *my* life, but rather that they will contribute more than the same period *typically* contributes to a person's lifetime well-being. So, for example, suppose I say I had a terrific childhood. Here, I might be saying, not that the events and experiences of my childhood will contribute more to my lifetime well-being than those of other times in my life, but that compared to the childhoods of many *other* people, the events and experiences of mine will make an especially large contribution to my lifetime well-being. That is, I might be making an *interpersonal comparative* claim.

A third possibility is that in saying somebody fared well during a particular period, we are saying that there were certain events in this person's life that will make a great *instrumental* contribution to their ultimate level of lifetime well-being. This person might, for example, have been promoted at work, learned a valuable lesson, recovered from an illness, had a rejuvenating holiday, etc. Even if none of these things will make an intrinsic contribution to this person's lifetime well-being, they might have paved the way for later events or experiences that will do so.

Which of these things we are in fact doing in such talk on a particular occasion will of course depend on the context and our intentions. Similarly, when we *ask* how somebody fared during a particular period, we might be asking about one or more of these things, depending on the context.

What about talk about good *futures*? I might say, for example, that I'm hoping that things go well for myself or others in the future. Here, I think we are usually saying that we hope the future of the person in question will contain a lot of the sort of events and experiences that make an intrinsic contribution to lifetime well-being.

Talk of momentary well-being

Switch now to talk of momentary well-being. Suppose I say 'Things are going well for me right now', or 'I'm faring really well at the moment'. What might I be trying to say? I might be trying to say that there have been a lot of things happening *recently* that will make a great contribution (either intrinsic or instrumental) to my ultimate lifetime well-being. I might be talking about their contributions *outright*. Alternatively, I might be talking about their contributions *relative to the events and experiences of other* (say, earlier) *times in my life*. Even if recent events in my life aren't making as great a contribution to my lifetime well-being as most people's life events do, still they might be making a much bigger contribution than earlier events in my life have made. Alternatively, I might be commenting on the contribution of these events *relative to my expectations*. So, I might be saying that they are contributing more than I had been expecting them to, or perhaps more than they might reasonably have been expected to.

Another possibility is that I am saying I am on track to achieving a high level of lifetime well-being. Here, I might be suggesting that it looks likely that I will end up with a high level of lifetime well-being (or perhaps a *higher* level relative to my earlier expectations or to reasonable expectations), or else (independently of what seems likely aside) *if* things continue to go in roughly the same sort of way they have been for me lately, then I will end up with a high level of lifetime well-being (or perhaps one that is higher than expected).

Again, which of these things I mean will vary with context, my intentions/goals in speaking here, and what has been asked of me.

Non-normative facts

Another thing we might be doing in such talk is asking about, or reporting on, certain non-normative facts or information. Suppose I ask how your holiday was. This might be shorthand for 'How was the hotel?', 'How was the weather?', 'Did you have fun activities?', or some combinations of these questions. It might be understood between us that the facts here sought to bear on your well-being, but also that I am just looking for the facts themselves.

Similarly, suppose someone asks me whether I had a good time at the party. They might be wanting to know simply whether I enjoyed myself, met interesting people, or whatever. That is, they might be seeking purely non-normative information such as this (for whatever purposes they happen to have).

Or suppose I ask how Jim is doing, knowing that he is in hospital. Here, I might simply be asking for information relating to his condition. Is he recovering? Is he feeling pain? And so on. I might not be asking about, or even interested in, his well-being at all – again, depending on the context.

Suppose Ryan hasn't seen Katie since high school. He bumps into a mutual acquaintance and asks how she is doing these days. He might well care about Katie, but here be simply asking for the material facts of her life since high school. Did she go to university? Is she married? What career did she go into? And so on. He might be curious just about these various things.

Suppose someone were to ask me whether I'd had 'a good childhood'. This might be their way of asking for certain non-normative information, such as whether I was healthy, loved by my parents, carefree, successful at school or in sports, and so on. Likewise, if I were to volunteer to someone that I'd had a terrific childhood, I might be attempting to communicate such non-normative facts as that in my childhood I was healthy, carefree, and so on.

Suppose I'm at a cafe and the waiter asks how I'm doing, and I respond 'I'm doing well, thanks'. This person might be seeking, and I might be commenting on, my mood alone. Here, I might just be saying that I'm in a good mood or feeling happy. In saying this, I needn't be implying anything about my well-being.

Reagan's question

Let's return to Bradley's case of Reagan. Can we understand and answer Reagan's question, if No Temporal Well-Being is true? Can I make sense of a request to comment on whether I am better off now than I was four years ago?

There are obvious ways of interpreting this question so that it makes sense without positing temporal well-being. Such a question might be asking whether recent events in my life now are contributing more to my lifetime well-being (either intrinsically or instrumentally) than events were four years ago. Alternatively, it might be asking whether I am now more likely than I was four years ago to be on track to achieving a high level of lifetime well-being. Alternatively, it might be asking for certain non-normative comparisons, such as whether I am healthier, wealthier, more successful in my career, etc., than I was four years ago. Whether Reagan himself was asking one of these things, something else meaningful, or alternatively a combination of these things, when he asked Americans this question is a matter for historians to debate. But one thing is likely: he was not asking us to reflect on the sort of thing that philosophers have in mind when they discuss or theorise about temporal well-being.

A final illustration

Suppose Susie is at a party and meets her friend, Jim. Susie asks Jim how their mutual friend, Paul, whom Susie has neither seen nor heard of for ten years, is doing nowadays. What might she be asking?

One possibility is that Susie is wanting to know whether Paul is roughly on track to achieving a high level of lifetime well-being. Are things (health, career, family, etc.) going for him in such a way that he is likely to end up well off in his life as a whole? Or better off than most people his age, in his position, or with his background? Or better off than it might have seemed ten years ago that he would end up?

Alternatively, Susie might be wanting to know, not about Paul's likely ultimate level of lifetime well-being, but about the level he *would* be likely to end up with if things keep going for him in roughly the way they have been lately (say, when it comes to his health, career, relationships, etc.).

Alternatively, Susie might be asking about *the intrinsic* contribution of recent events and experiences in Paul's life to his ultimate level of lifetime well-being. Has Jim been having a lot of things happen to him lately that will, at the end of his life, count for a great deal toward how good his life considered as a whole was for him? Such things might include, for example, wonderful pleasures, intellectual stimulation, momentous achievements, and so on.

Once we are clear on all these different possible interpretations of talk about how people are faring either at times or over periods of time, I suspect we will be much less inclined to posit or believe in something like temporal well-being.

4.5 The vindication objection

The next objection I want to consider is that in providing all these possible interpretations of the relevant talk, I have succeeded in showing, not that temporal well-being does not exist, but rather what it *is* (and so precisely that it does exist).

Velleman suggests (though does not accept) a view of momentary well-being on which

> the only way to assess someone's well-being at a particular moment [is] to compute the fraction of his life's value that was being realized at the time.[7]

Lifetime well-being comes first, and then temporal well-being is derived from it. Am I not suggesting something similar – i.e., that one is doing well at a certain time just in case recent events and experiences in one's life will make a great contribution to one's eventual lifetime well-being?

No. As I pointed out in Chapter 2, well-being is intrinsically normatively significant for us. None of the things I've suggested we are talking about when we are talking about how people are doing or faring at moments or over periods is normatively significant in *this* way. For example, that it is likely, at a certain time, that I will end up with a high level of lifetime well-being is not itself intrinsically normatively significant. The ultimate source of my self-interested reasons is just my lifetime well-being, not facts about whether it is likely that I will end up with a high level of lifetime well-being.

4.6 A life worth living

It might be objected that if No Temporal Well-Being is true, then we cannot make sense of talk of whether someone's life is worth living (for her[8]) or not. Somebody's life is worth living at a certain time, it might be suggested, just in case her momentary well-being then is greater than zero. If it is at a neutral level or less than zero, then it is not worth living – there is a sense in which she would be better off dead. If one were to see a poor animal suffering greatly and comment 'that's not a life worth living', what else could one mean except that this animal's current level of momentary well-being is negative?

I think this is the wrong way to understand talk of whether a life is worth living or not. Such talk is better understood in other ways. For example, one thing we might mean when we say that someone's life is worth living at a certain time is just that *if she were to live on, then her lifetime well-being would end up higher, all things considered (i.e., not simply in certain respects), than if she were to die now.* We might say this, for example, of somebody who, though she is severely depressed right now, will recover and flourish if she lives on.

A different thing we might mean when we say that someone's life is worth living at a certain time is that if she were to live on *in a similar state to that which she is in right now* – say, when it comes to things like her mental or physical health, ability to move freely, level of happiness, and so on – then she would end up with a higher level of lifetime well-being than if she were to die now. We might say this, for example, of somebody whose physical or mental health is compromised, but not so greatly that carrying on in roughly that state would prevent her from making further increases in her lifetime well-being.

Can we meaningfully talk or ask about whether someone's life was worth living *considered as a whole* (i.e., whether she was better off having lived this life than living no life at all)? I doubt it, but I will not go into this matter here.

Notes

1 See, for example, McMahan (2002), p. 180.
2 See, for example, Rawls (1971). For useful discussion of such a view, see Heathwood (2011).
3 Bradley (2009), p. 74. My emphasis.

4 Bradley's own solution – ingenious, though in my view, mistaken – to this timing puzzle is to try to show that death makes us worse off at times *after* we are dead. See Bradley (2009).
5 Bradley (2009), p. 89.
6 Bradley (2016).
7 Velleman (2000), p. 57.
8 We should distinguish between a life worth living for one, and a life worth living in other senses. For more on this distinction, see Bramble (2014b).

References

Bradley, B. (2009). *Well-Being and Death*. Oxford: Oxford University Press.
Bradley, B. (2016). Well-Being at a Time. *Philosophic Exchange* 45(1).
Bramble, B. (2014b). On William James's 'Is Life Worth Living?'. *Ethics* 125(1): 217–219.
Heathwood, C. (2011). Preferentism and Self Sacrifice. *Pacific Philosophical Quarterly* 92(1): 18–38.
McMahan, J. (2002). *The Ethics of Killing*. Oxford: Oxford University Press.
Rawls, J. (1971). *A Theory of Justice*. Cambridge, MA: Harvard University Press.
Velleman, D. (2000). Well-being and Time. Reprinted in *The Possibility of Practical Reason*. Oxford: Oxford University Press, pp. 56–84.

5 Conclusion and implications

In this book, I have argued for No Temporal Well-Being, the view that there is no such thing as temporal well-being. There is only one genuine kind of well-being: lifetime well-being. I have given two independent arguments for this view. The first, The Normative Significance Argument, went like this: If momentary and periodic well-being were kinds of well-being, then they should have *intrinsic* normative significance for us – that is, their normative significance for us should not be exhausted by their relevance or implications for *something else* (for example, lifetime well-being). They should have significance for us *independently* of any such implications. But only lifetime well-being can have intrinsic normative significance. So, temporal well-being does not exist.

The second argument, The No Credible Theories Argument, claimed that there are no credible theories of temporal well-being, and that the best explanation of this is that there is no genuine phenomenon here to account for.

I then responded to six important objections to this view, in part by explaining what our everyday talk about well-being at moments and during periods is really about, if not what philosophers have in mind by temporal well-being. Most such talk, I claimed, is about the contributions of events and experiences during such moments and periods toward lifetime well-being, and not about some other kind of well-being, one occurring at the times in question.

Suppose No Temporal Well-Being is true, what follows from it? Why is its truth something that should be regarded as interesting or important? In the rest of this conclusion, I will attempt to answer these questions.

5.1 Wasted theorising

If No Temporal Well-Being is true, then philosophers are wasting a great deal of time theorising about the nature of temporal well-being. Their efforts are doomed to failure, since there is nothing here to give a theory of.

Moreover, philosophers are wasting their time trying to work out how lifetime well-being is constructed out of temporal well-being. Lifetime well-being *cannot* be constructed out of temporal well-being, since there is no such thing as temporal well-being. To take one example, an uphill life *cannot* be better for one, other things equal, than a downhill life. The question of whether it is, is simply ill-conceived. Lives don't have shapes or directions, at least not shapes or directions of something like momentary well-being. Similarly, debates about temporal neutrality – i.e., about whether temporal benefits later in life add more to lifetime well-being than temporal benefits earlier in life do – are empty.[1]

Philosophers are also wasting their time trying to solve the timing problem for the badness of death. It is a pseudo-problem. There is no problem of how death can harm us without making us worse off at some time, since there is no such thing as well-being at a time. *Nothing* can make us worse off at a time. We do not have well-being at times for death to potentially reduce.

What about the graphs mentioned in Chapter 1 that are used to depict momentary well-being over the course of a life? These should be done away with. They cannot represent what philosophers and economists intend for them to represent, since there is no such thing as momentary well-being. We cannot map well-being in this way.[2] For these reasons, we cannot calculate lifetime well-being by calculating the area under the curve in such a graph.

5.2 Childhood well-being

There is a lively debate going on at the moment among philosophers about the value for us of childhood. As Gheaus nicely characterises the debate, some philosophers think that childhood is valuable 'only instrumentally, in preparation for adulthood'.[3] According to these philosophers, 'if we had the choice to skip childhood and come into the world as fully formed adults',[4] it might be rational to do so. By contrast, others, such as Gheaus herself, hold that 'childhood is intrinsically good',[5] or that 'some of childhood's own goods – that is, things that are necessary for a good childhood – also have intrinsic value, rather than being merely instrumental for subsequent stages of life'.[6] Another who holds a view like Gheaus's is Brennan, who argues that 'there are childhood goods with a value that goes beyond their instrumental value'.[7] She writes:

> I think it's a deeply mistaken and pervasive view of parenting that our main obligations consist in shepherding our children safely to the threshold of adulthood, well prepared for autonomous adult lives. Such a view neglects the importance of the goods both parents and children get from childhood itself.[8]

I agree with both Gheaus and Brennan that what goes on during our childhood is not valuable for us purely for its effects on our *adulthood*. But I think they err in thinking of children as having levels of well-being themselves. Things can indeed go well or poorly for children – but only *qua* the larger individuals who merely happen, at these times, to have been children.[9] They cannot go well or poorly for children *qua* children. It is not as if children are, in their identities, in some way distinct from, or independent of, the individuals whose lives as wholes will end up including their childhoods as parts. So, while Gheaus and Brennan are right that what goes on during our childhood is not valuable for us purely for its effects on our *adulthood*, it is nonetheless true that what goes on during childhood is valuable for us purely for its implications for something else, our *lifetime* well-being.

The implications in question can be either causal or constitutive. By their being causal, I mean that events in childhood can make a difference to what happens in adulthood, where it is these occurrences in adulthood that make an intrinsic difference to lifetime well-being. By their being constitutive, I mean that events in childhood can themselves make an intrinsic difference to one's lifetime well-being, independently of any effects they might have on what happens after childhood.

How can events in childhood make an intrinsic difference to lifetime well-being? The main way, it seems to me, is through their *uniqueness* – or, more precisely, the qualitative uniqueness of the associated pleasures. There are certain kinds of pleasures, that is, that are available *only* in childhood. Brennan does a nice job of explaining the sort of pleasures I have in mind:

> Despite the rise of play therapy for adults and discussions of making peace with one's inner child, there seems to be something unique about play as a good of childhood. There also seems to be something distinctive about childhood friendships and relationships. Friends play a different sort of role in childhood than they do in later life and people report feeling an attachment to childhood friends out of all proportion to the sorts of shared interests and beliefs that usually form the basis of adult friendships. There is also a sense of time as endless, as having one's whole life stretched out ahead (think too of endless summer vacations) that one never has again in life. Likewise, there is the sense that all doors are open and that anything is possible. This sense fades as one leaves childhood. Finally, there is a kind of absolute trust in others, possible in childhood but then never again.[10]

Brennan herself isn't thinking of the value of these things purely in terms of pleasures. But it seems to me that we can most plausibly explain what is so valuable in these events and experiences in terms of the associated pleasures. If you miss out on these pleasures in childhood, you will not have a chance to experience them again. This places a limit on how good your life as a whole can be for you.[11]

This way of thinking of things, I believe, helps a great deal in reconciling the above approaches. It explains the sense in which childhood is not valuable in itself – there is, after all, no such thing as childhood well-being that could be worth promoting independently of its implications for something else – while at the same time explaining why the events and experiences of childhood are not valuable for us solely for their contribution to our adulthood.

5.3 Public policy

Many public policies are aimed at making people as well off as possible. Such policy-making often appeals, either implicitly or explicitly, to momentary well-being. It asks 1) how well off people are *right now* (i.e., at the present moment), and then 2) how we can make them better off at future times.

If No Temporal Well-Being is true, however, this way of making policy is mistaken. What we should be doing instead is thinking about how to make individuals as well off as possible in their lives considered as wholes. Right now, given the way things are, there are facts about how well off people are going to end up in their lives considered as wholes. We should make policy that increases these lifetime values.[12] If policy-makers are going to achieve the right results, it is vital that they self-consciously think this way, that policy not be aimed at making us better off at times, but rather in our lives as wholes.[13]

In targeting improved outcomes for our citizens, we need to realise that these are extended beings with whole lives that will be theirs. The goal should not be getting them to a certain state and sustaining them there, but rather their having a certain life trajectory, including certain things happening over time, perhaps in a certain order, or with a certain relationship to each other.

To illustrate the difference here, I want to consider three different kinds of policies, policies concerning 1) children, 2) the gravely ill, 3) the worst off among us. Let us start with children. As I noted above, Skelton writes:

> The nature of children's welfare is of great relevance to a host of moral, political, and practical questions relating to the treatment of children.[14]

Brennan, too, writes:

> An important question facing parents is how do we, as agents who act on behalf of children, balance things that are good for the child-as-child

with the things that are good for the child-as-future-adult? It's my hope that seeing the obligations that parents have towards children in this way demonstrates what a complex and creative task parenting can be. While parenting becomes more demanding than the old-fashioned 'deliver them safely to the threshold of their adult years' approach, I also think the ways in which it's more demanding show how engaging an endeavour parenthood can be.[15]

If there is no such thing as temporal well-being, then it is a problem if policy-makers are thinking of children as possessing something like temporal well-being, something worth promoting independently of the lifetime well-being of the individual who is, at this time, a child (i.e., independently of how the events and experiences of childhood fit into a larger whole). While it is true that they shouldn't be thinking just of how childhood events and experiences contribute to the adults we become, they should be thinking just about the contribution of these events and experiences to the value of the life as a whole.

Let's take a concrete case. Here is Bagattini and MacLeod:

> Physicians and social workers sometimes seek to protect children from their parents. Yet parents often view interventions into the private life of the family as meddlesome and destructive. In such disputes, *both sides appeal to the well-being of children to justify their actions*. How should such conflicts be adjudicated? How are the choices and preferences of children relevant to tracking their interests? In the face of a plurality of interpretations of child well-being, what conception of well-being should a just state employ to craft effective laws and public policies that bear upon the treatment of children? Credible answers to these and related questions depend on identifying and assessing the significance of distinct dimensions of children's well-being.[16]

Bagattini and MacLeod are right that we need a way of adjudicating such disputes, and that this should involve an appeal to people's interests. But if there is no such thing as temporal well-being, then we are liable to get the wrong answers if we are thinking in terms of childhood well-being. Instead, we should be thinking about the whole lives that are likely to end up as these individuals' given the different options. We need to look, in other words, to the long term.

The point of a lot of these theorists is that we need to consider a person's well-being *as a child*. I agree that we need to consider more than just the impact of childhood on one's adulthood, but to understand this additional thing we need still to think about the long term – specifically, one's life considered as a whole. This is because the relevant contribution of the events and experiences of one's childhood will be a contribution to one's lifetime well-being, for this is the only well-being one will have. We should be thinking about what sort of things we want a person to experience or to have happen to her in childhood if she is to have the best whole life that is possible for her. We must be careful not to fetishise childhood, by divorcing it in our imagination from our whole lives.

Consider, next, the gravely ill, and decisions about the allocation of scarce medical resources. Broome rightly says:

> The health service has to decide what treatments it should make available to patients with a terminal disease. Should it give priority to building hospices that offer palliative care, or to the resources that are needed for more aggressive treatment? So it is an inescapable practical problem to try and judge which is the right treatment to choose.[17]

But then he goes on:

> I shall use diagrams of a particular sort to illustrate one aspect of problems like this. Figure 1 [Figure 5.1] is the first of them.[18]

If such graphs, however, are nonsense, then they will not be a useful guide to answering these important practical questions. It might help instead to think of graphs depicting not well-being on the y axis, but, say, pain.

It is no use to think about these people's well-being at times, and try to extract from this some way of working out what is best for people. What we need to be thinking about instead is how much extra time for people who are gravely suffering is likely to add to their lifetime well-being. It is contributions toward lifetime well-being, the value of likely whole-lives, that we must be thinking about, that must guide our policy-decisions on such matters.

Consider, finally, policy-making concerning the worst off among us. Some people think that 'Benefiting people matters more the worse off these people are.'[19] If No Temporal Well-Being is true, however, then we need to rethink what this could mean. It couldn't mean that people have levels of momentary well-being, and that it is better to increase the momentary well-being of those who are at lower levels. Perhaps we could still attach some sense to it if we interpreted it as meaning this: It is better to do what would increase the lifetime well-being of those whose lifetime well-being is going to be lower.

Summing up, policy should indeed be aimed at maximising well-being (at least some of the time), and so we need to know how to measure well-being.

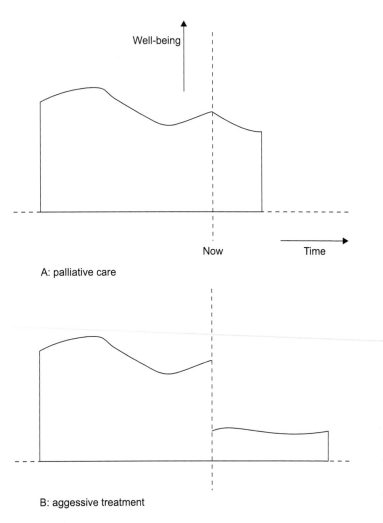

Figure 5.1 Treatments for a terminal disease

Adapted from 'Figure 1. Treatments for a terminal disease'. Broome, J. (2004). *Weighing Lives*. Oxford: Oxford University Press.

The fact that only lifetime well-being exists, then, is a critical insight. How *do* we measure well-being? My suggestion has been that we focus on the versions of the best theories of lifetime well-being that do not attempt to construct lifetime well-being out of temporal well-being (see Chapter 4 for details).

5.4 National prosperity

Many people now think that we should be measuring the prosperity of nations in terms of the well-being of these nations' citizens. This is a very plausible view. However, there is a risk that such measurement will be done incorrectly if we are thinking of well-being in the wrong way. In particular, we cannot succeed in measuring prosperity by trying to work out how well off people are *right now* (i.e., at the present moment). There is no fact about *this*. Instead, what we should be trying to measure is the likely lifetime well-being of citizens who are living right now (perhaps with a special focus on the young).

5.5 Dangers of believing in temporal well-being

Suppose I am right, and there is no such thing as temporal well-being. It follows, trivially, that if you believe in temporal well-being, you have a false belief, and that if you're theorising about it, you're engaged in a futile endeavour. But there is a more insidious consequence. If you think that temporal well-being exists, *you are likely to think that it has intrinsic normative significance*. After all, as I've claimed, well-being is, as a conceptual matter, the sort of thing that has intrinsic normative significance. So, if you think that temporal well-being exists, you're naturally inclined to think that it matters in and of itself, is worth measuring, informing policy with, etc. These thoughts could mislead policy-makers, and result in worse outcomes for us all.

Believing in temporal well-being might also incline one to misunderstand the value of living in the moment. Living in the moment has value for us because it can result in special experiences – say, certain kinds of flow pleasures – that can, at least on certain occasions, make great intrinsic contributions to our lifetime well-being. It does not have value for us independently of this. If you think that there is such a thing as momentary well-being, and that it matters for us in and of itself, you might be inclined to miss this truth and try to get high and stay high, ignoring the long-term trajectory or bigger picture of one's life.

You might also be more inclined to think that extra years are good for one no matter what one is feeling then, so long as it is pleasurable. Why? Because this would be extra momentary well-being, after all, and momentary well-being is worth promoting. The reality, however, might be that one's feeling good in these extra years adds nothing or little to one's lifetime well-being, if, say, it is pleasure that brings nothing qualitatively new in terms of pleasurableness to one's life.

Finally, you might be less inclined to consider or take seriously the idea that certain pleasures can fail to be good for us at all, and that certain pains can fail to be bad for us at all. 'Surely all pleasures and pains affect our well-being, if only our *momentary* well-being!', you might think, and so conclude, without justification, that they must have some normative significance for us.

5.6   QALYS versus WELBYS/WALYS

As Broome explains,

> Health economists . . . commonly measure the benefits of treatment in terms of 'quality-adjusted life years', or qalys. A person's quality-adjusted life years are the number of years she lives, adjusted for their quality. 'Quality' refers to the quality of the person's health only. For example, a quality of life might be: in constant slight pain and unable to walk. Another might be: deaf. A year in good health counts as one qaly. A year in less good health counts as less than one qaly; its value is reduced by a 'quality-adjustment factor'. If a particular quality has an adjustment factor of .7, a year of life at that quality would be valued at .7 of a qaly, equivalent to .7 of a year in good health. To calculate a person's qalys, we add up across the years of her life, counting each year at its quality-adjustment factor. Take the example of [aggressive versus palliative treatment]. . . . Aggressive treatment will lead to the patient's having some number of qalys, and palliative treatment to her having a different number. A health economist would favour the treatment that leads to the greater number of qalys.

Some, including economists and bodies such as the UK Medical Research Council, are exploring ways of improving or replacing QALYs. One suggestion has been to use well-being to value outcomes by developing a 'well-being-adjusted life-year' (WELBY or WALY).[20] This would be a kind of temporal well-being. As Broome puts it, 'A person's qalys are formally parallel to the total of her temporal wellbeing, added up through her life.'[21] He goes on:

> In health economics the data are concerned with health only. A person's health is a component of her wellbeing, but not all of her wellbeing. So in using qalys, health economists are deliberately attending to only one part of wellbeing. I think they are wrong to do so. But I mention qalys because I think they represent something like the right approach to the problem of weighing lives. The approach would be exactly right if wellbeing were substituted for quality of life as health economists understand it. Qalys simply need to be generalized. We need wellbeing-adjusted life years instead of quality-adjusted life years.[22]

Ben Todd, CEO and co-founder of the effective altruist organisation 80,000 Hours, writes:

> I often see media coverage of effective altruism that says 'effective altruists want to maximise the number of QALYs in the world'. . . . This is wrong. QALYs only measure health, and health is not all that matters. Most effective altruists care about increasing the number of 'WALYs' or well-being adjusted life years, where health is just one component of wellbeing.[23]

I am all for policy decisions being guided by the effects of the relevant policies on well-being. But I think that replacing QALYS with WELBYS would be a bad idea. We need to think instead of the effects of policies on the well-being of lives considered as wholes. This will be harder to measure, but it must be done this way if we going to formulate policy that will best improve outcomes.

5.7 The final word

Am I proposing we stop talking and asking about how people are faring at times and during periods such as childhood? No. There is no harm in continuing to talk this way, provided we do not allow ourselves to be misled by the surface grammar of such talk into thinking that we are here attributing to people a state that they can be in at times that has normative significance independently of its implications for lifetime well-being. Most people are not liable to be misled in this way. It is mainly philosophers, and other kinds of theorists, who might be misled in this way. So, provided we understand that such talk should not be construed literally, there is no problem. It is fine for us to keep saying things like 'I had a good childhood' and 'How is John faring these days?' in just the same way it is fine for us to talk about how our car or plant is doing, even though cars and plants can have well-being in only a metaphorical sense.

Notes

1 Though one can meaningfully debate whether the temporal location of, say, a pleasure makes a difference to its intrinsic contribution to lifetime well-being.
2 Though perhaps there are other features of lives we can interestingly map.
3 Gheaus (2015), p. 35.
4 Gheaus (2015), p. 35.
5 Gheaus (2015), p. 36.
6 Gheaus (2015), p. 36.
7 Brennan (2014), p. 43.

8 Brennan (2014), p. 44.
9 An exception, of course, is those who never make it to adulthood. For these individuals, their lives as wholes are the same as their childhoods.
10 Brennan (2014), p. 43.
11 For more on the value of qualitatively unique pleasures, see Bramble (2016).
12 I leave out the important matter of the non-identity problem here.
13 Compare Broome's 'snapshot approach' vs. 'people approach' to aggregation. See Broome (2004).
14 Skelton (2015), p. 367.
15 Brennan (2014), p. 44.
16 Bagattini and Macleod (2015).
17 Broome (2004), p. 2.
18 Broome (2004), p. 2.
19 Parfit (1997), p. 213.
20 Brazier and Tsuchiya (2015).
21 Broome (2004), p. 261.
22 Broome (2004), p. 261.
23 http://effective-altruism.com/ea/pu/we_care_about_walys_not_qalys/

References

Bagattini, A. and Macleod, C. (2015). *The Nature of Children's Well-Being*. Dordrecht: Springer.

Bramble, B. (2016). A New Defense of Hedonism About Well-Being. *Ergo* 3(4). DOI: http://dx.doi.org/10.3998/ergo.12405314.0003.004

Brazier, J. and Tsuchiya, A. (2015). Improving Cross-Sector Comparisons: Going Beyond the Health-Related QALY. *Applied Health Economics and Health Policy* 13(6): 557–565.

Brennan, S. (2014). The Goods of Childhood and Children's Rights. In: F. Baylis and C. Macleod (eds.), *Family Making: Contemporary Ethical Challenges*. Oxford: Oxford University Press.

Broome, J. (2004). *Weighing Lives*. Oxford: Oxford University Press.

Gheaus, A. (2015). The 'Intrinsic Goods of Childhood' and the Just Society. In: A. Bagattini and C. Macleod (eds.), *The Nature of Children's Well-Being*. Dordrecht: Springer.

Parfit, D. (1997). Equality and Priority. *Ratio* 10(3): 202–201.

Skelton, A. (2015). Children's Well-Being: A Philosophical Analysis. In: Guy Fletcher (ed.), *The Routledge Handbook of Philosophy of Well-Being*. London: Routledge, pp. 366–377.

Index

Bradley, B. 2, 8, 19–20, 23, 29, 34, 36, 43–45
Broome, J. 3, 7, 34, 57–58, 60

childhood well-being 5–10, 16–17, 20–22, 34–36, 42, 45–48, 53–57
concept of well-being 1, 13–14

desire-based theories 37–38, 42
Dorsey, D. 4, 7–8, 35–36

events 43–44

future well-being 19–20, 22–25, 46, 55–56

hedonism 8, 29–33, 41–42

internalism 34–38, 44

life worth living 50

national prosperity 59

objective list theories 33–37, 42–43

pain 22–25, 29–33, 41–44, 47, 57, 59–60
pleasure 3, 29–33, 41–43, 47, 49, 54–55, 59–60
public policy 55–59, 61

QALYS 60–61

reasons for action 13–15, 19–20, 22–28, 34–36

shape of a life 8–9, 53

Velleman, D. 3–4, 8, 17–18, 25–27, 34, 49